Pooping Animals

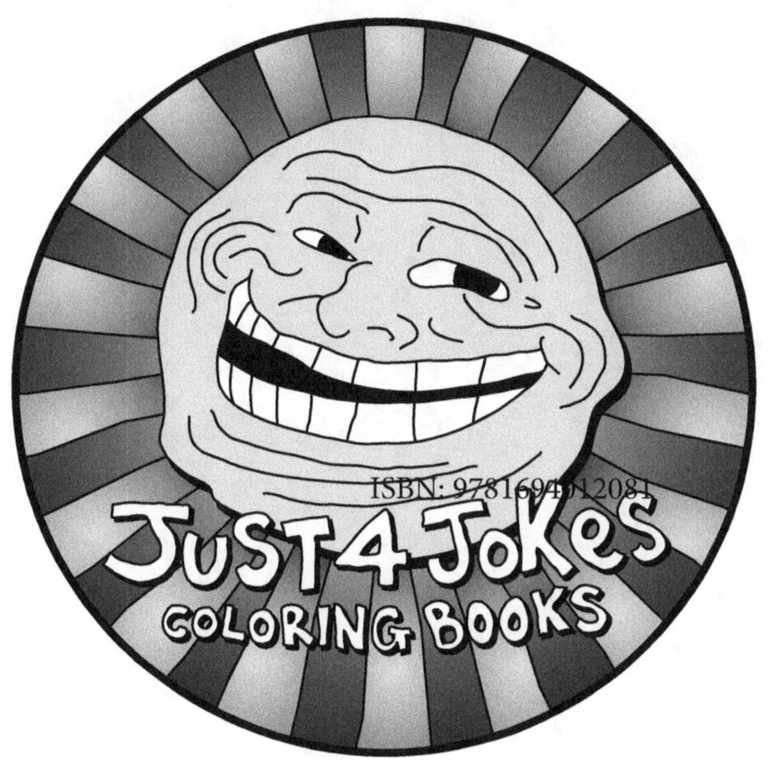

ISBN: 9781694012081

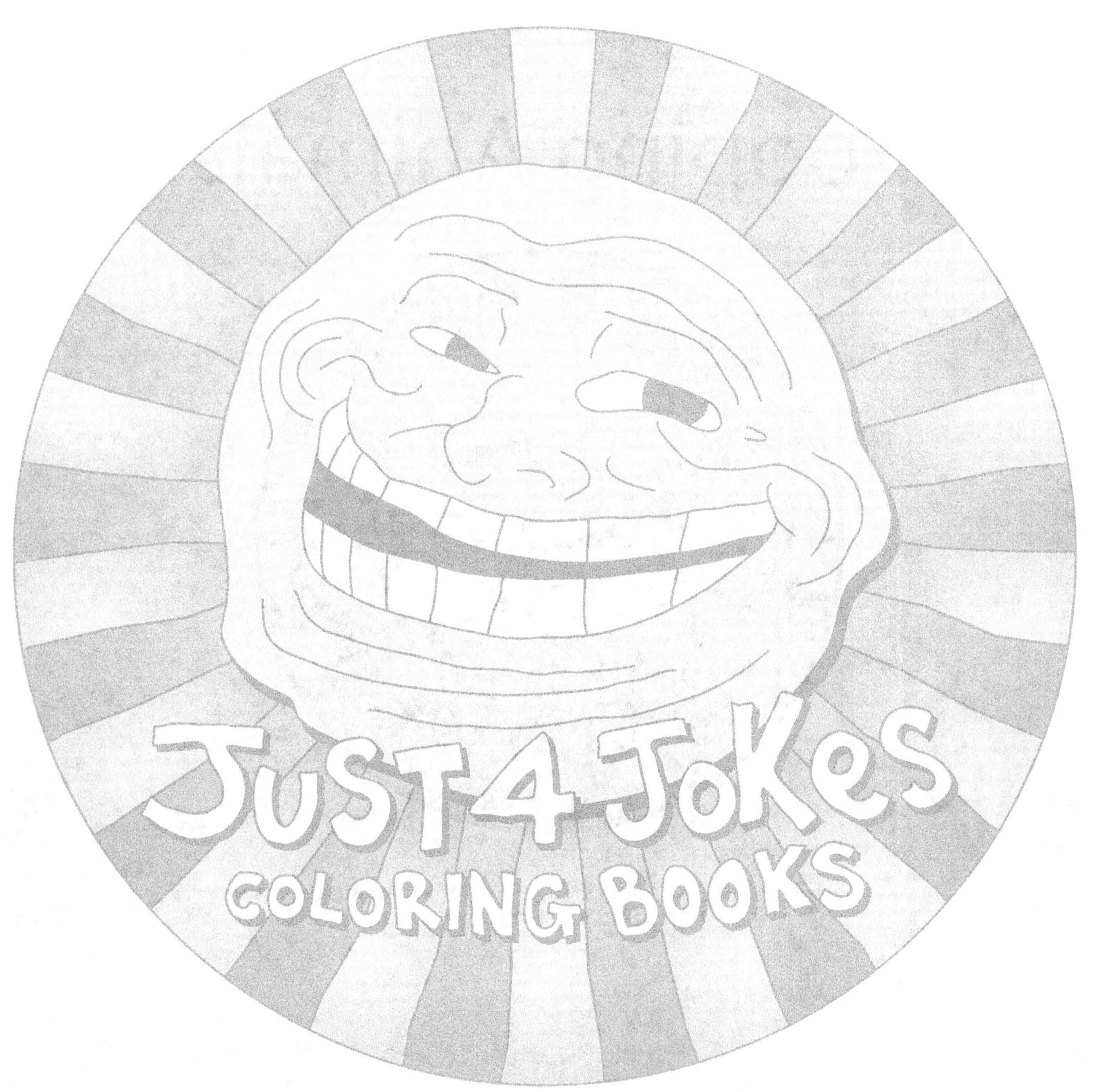

Just 4 Jokes
COLORING BOOKS

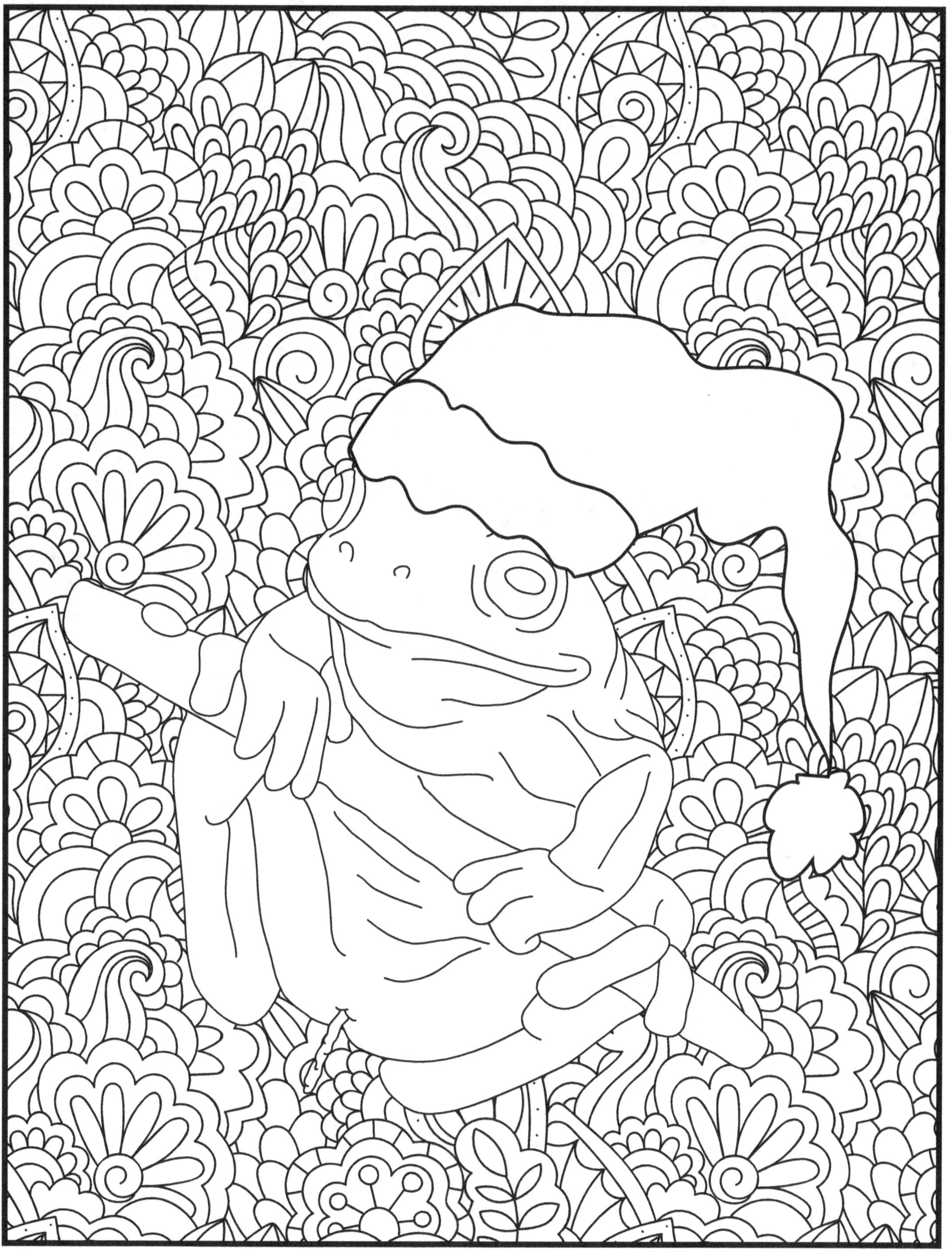

JUST 4 JOKES
COLORING BOOKS

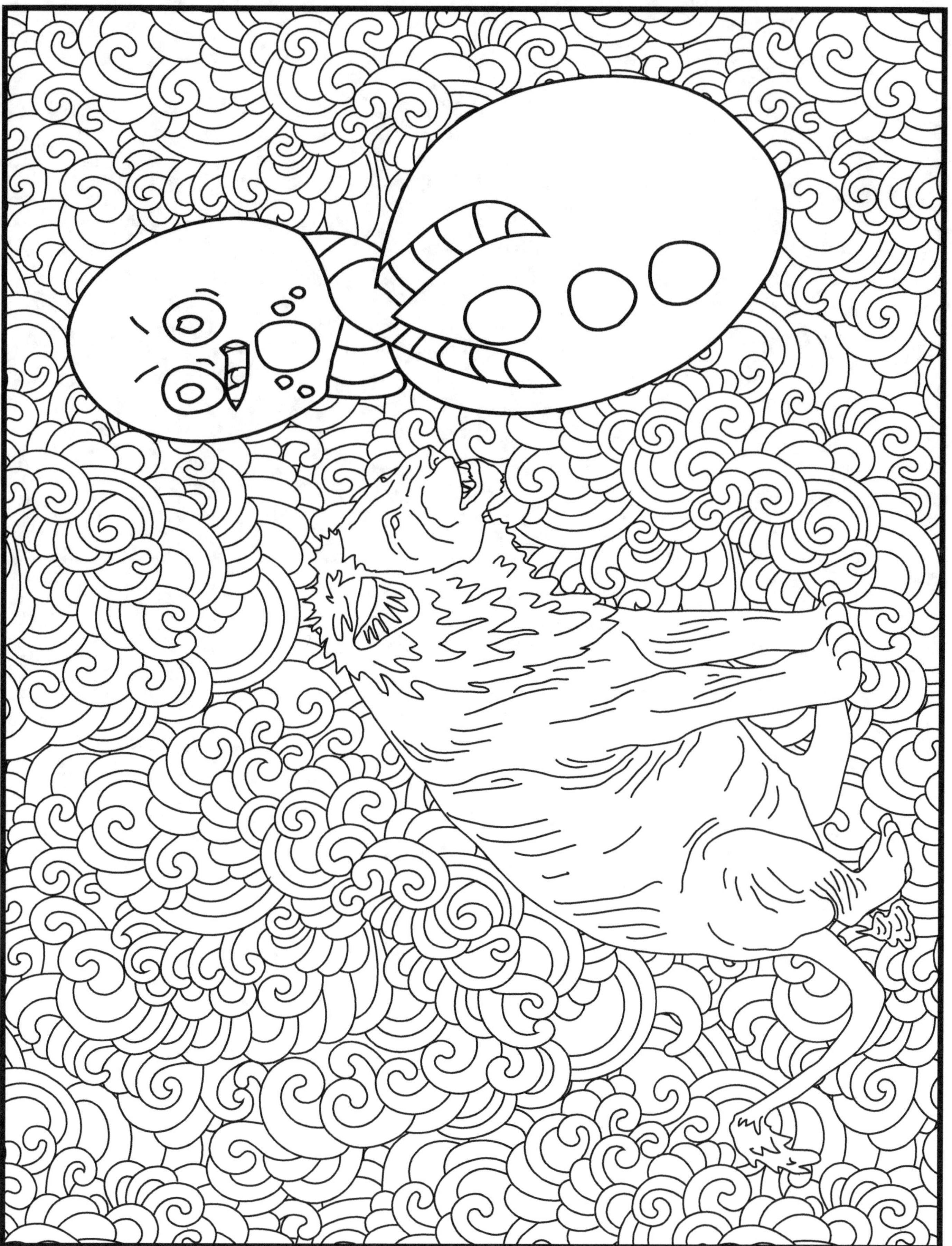

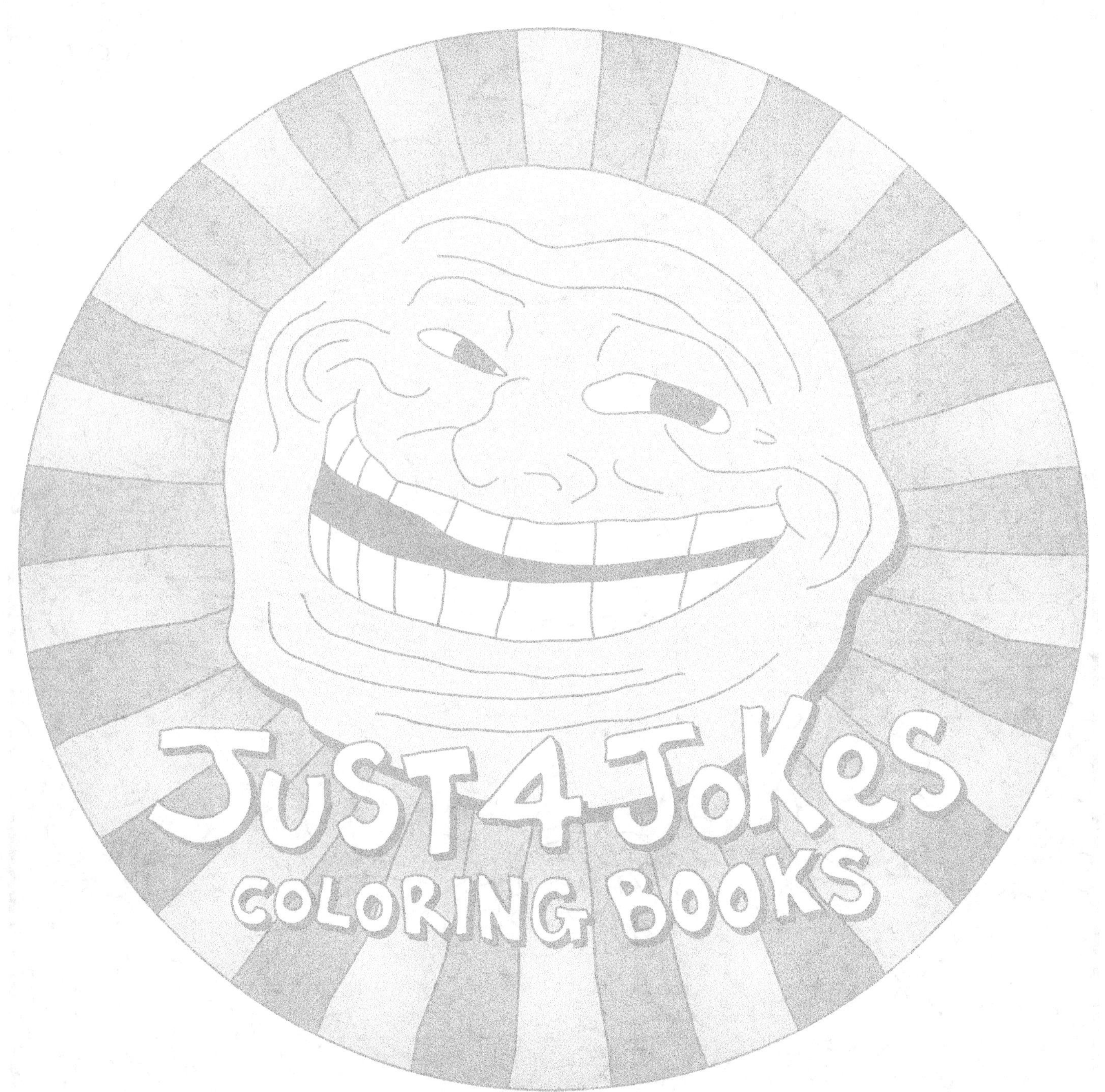

Just 4 Jokes
COLORING BOOKS

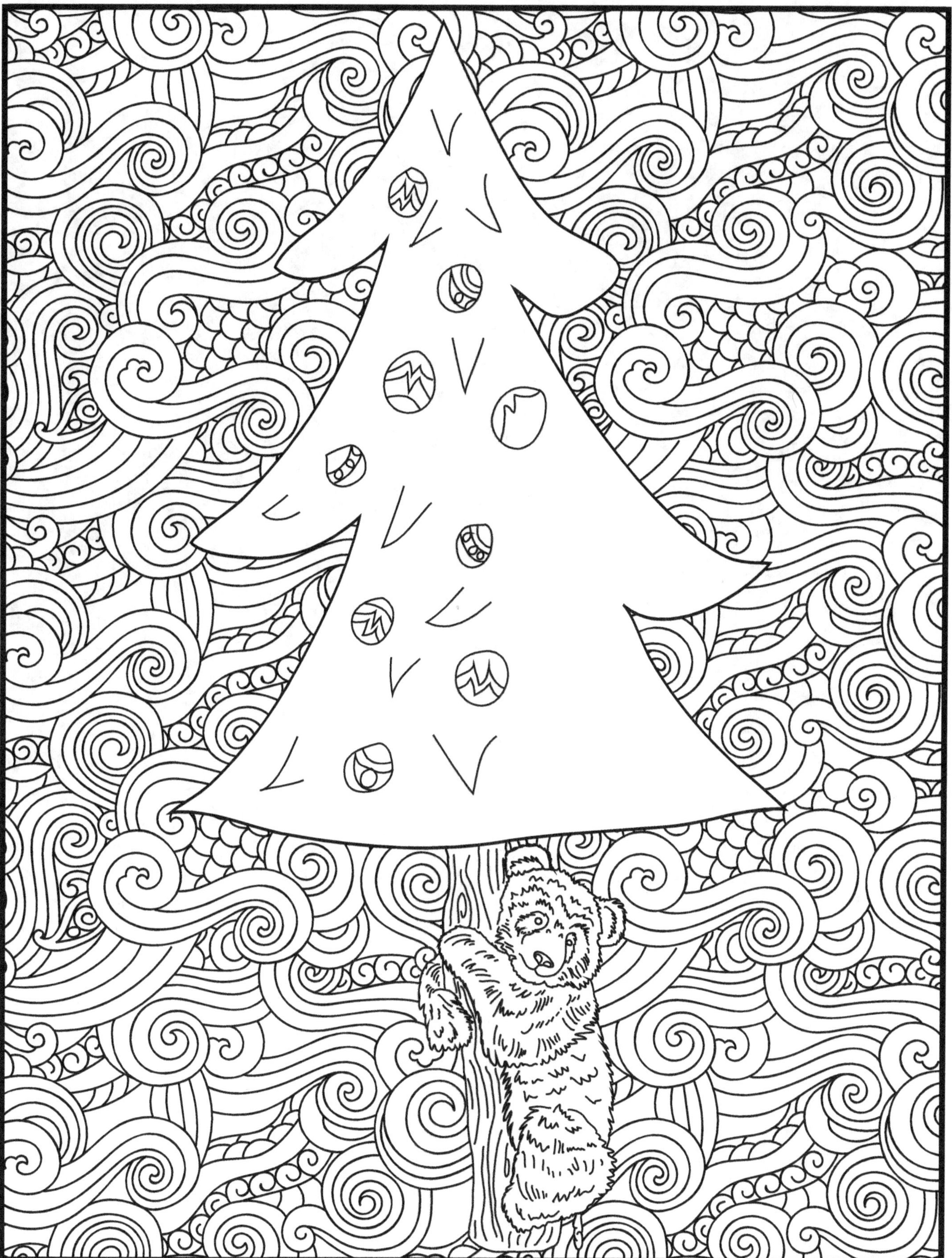

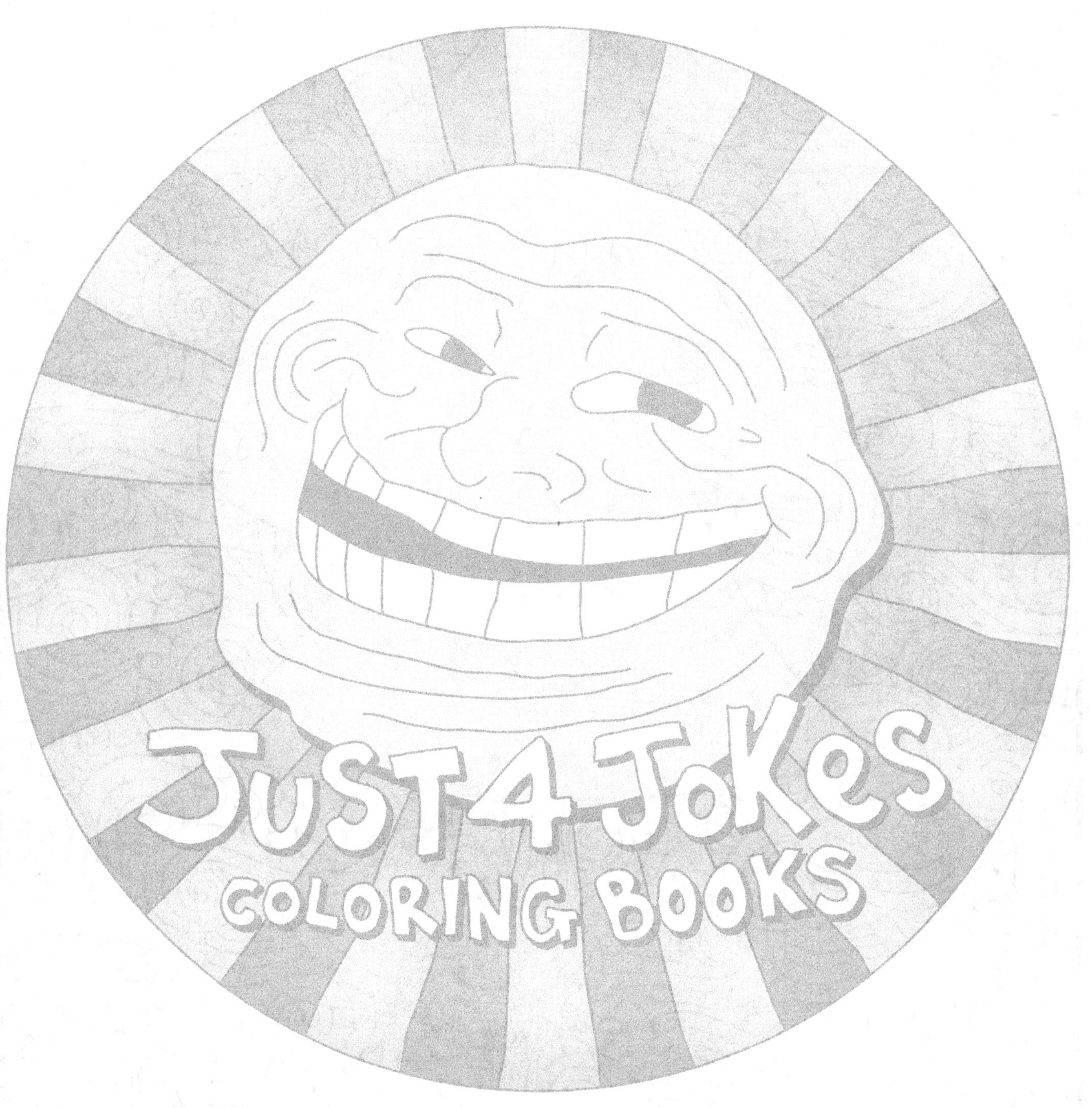

JUST 4 JOKES
COLORING BOOKS

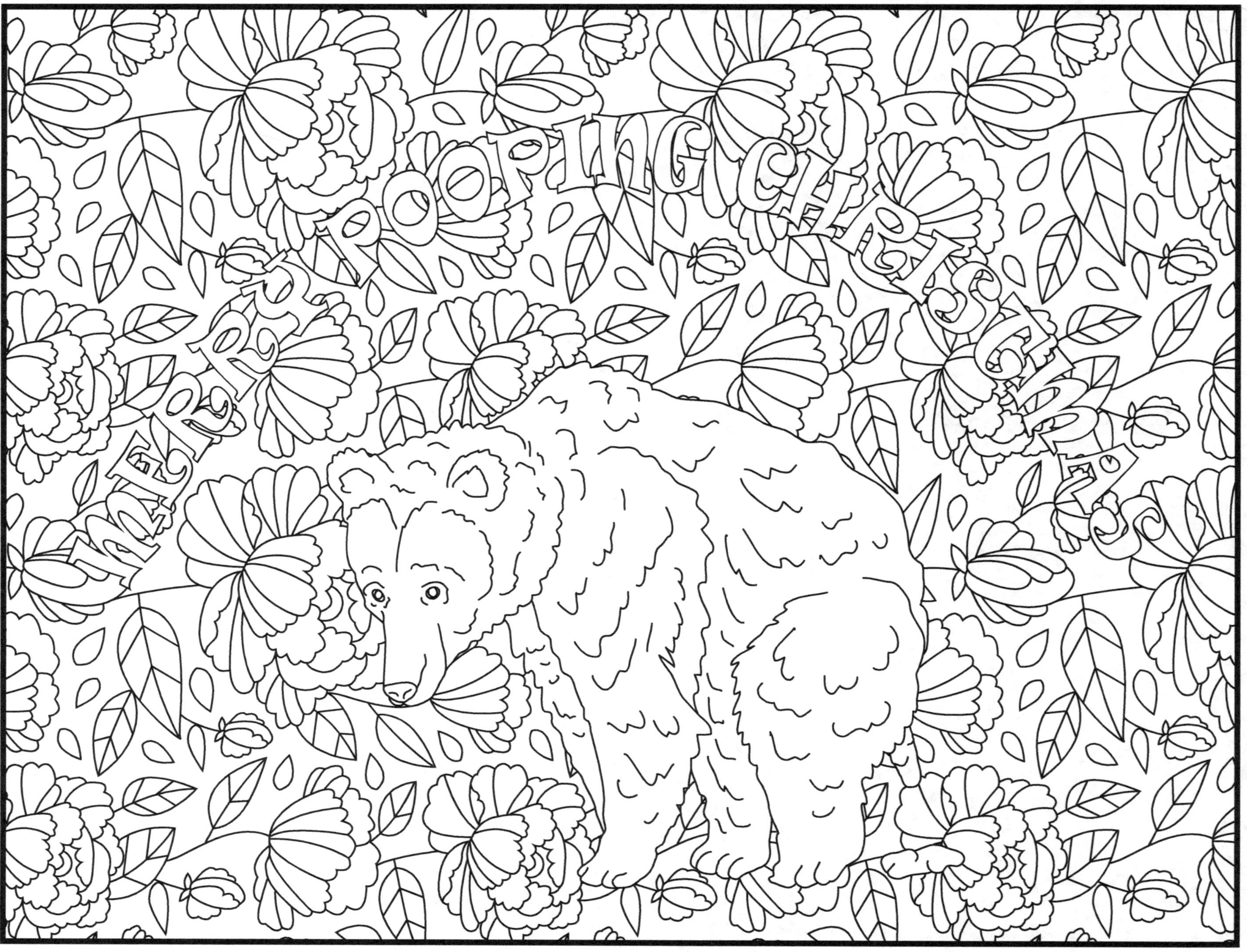

MERRY POOPING CHRISTMAS

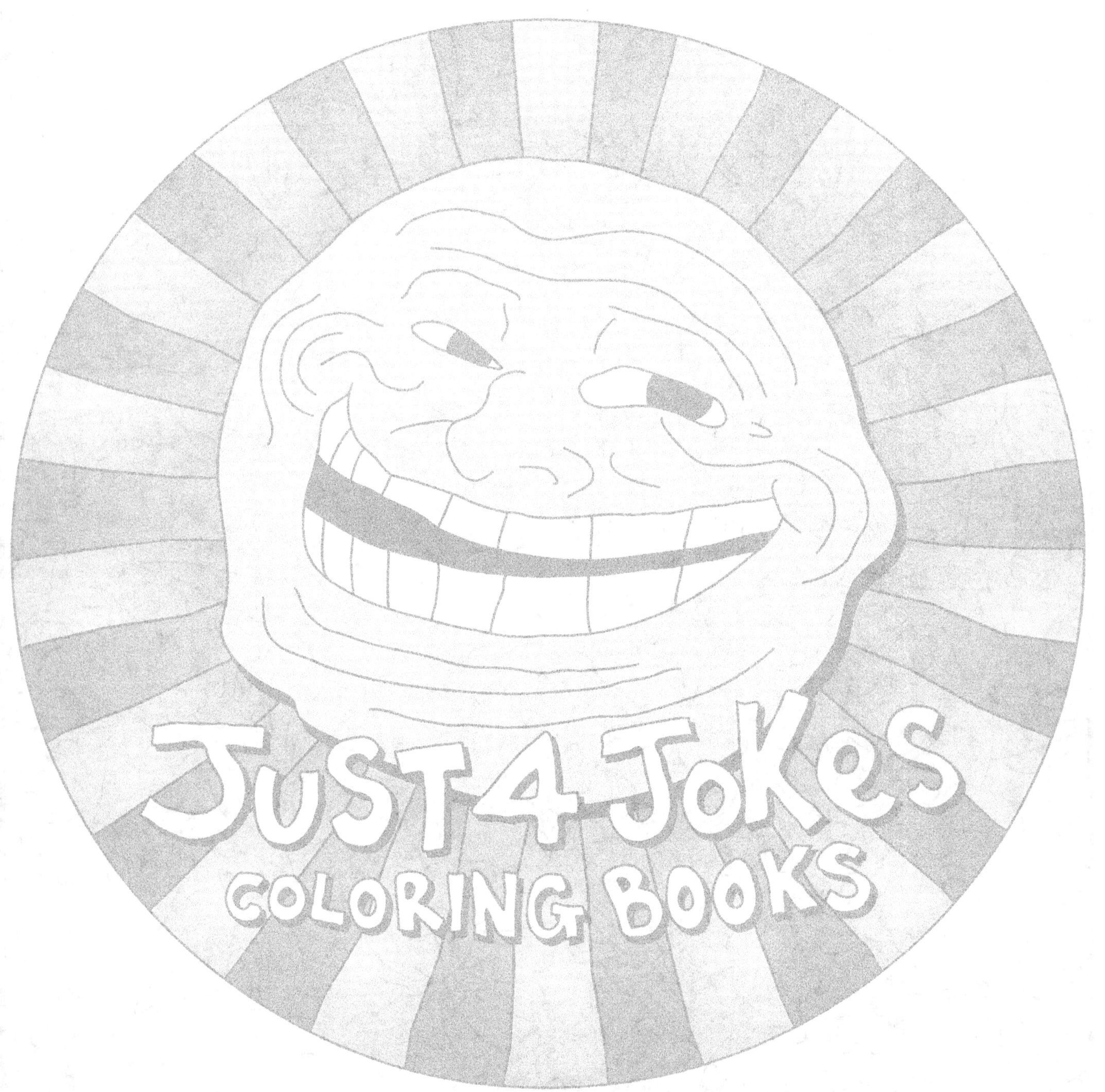

Just4Jokes
COLORING BOOKS

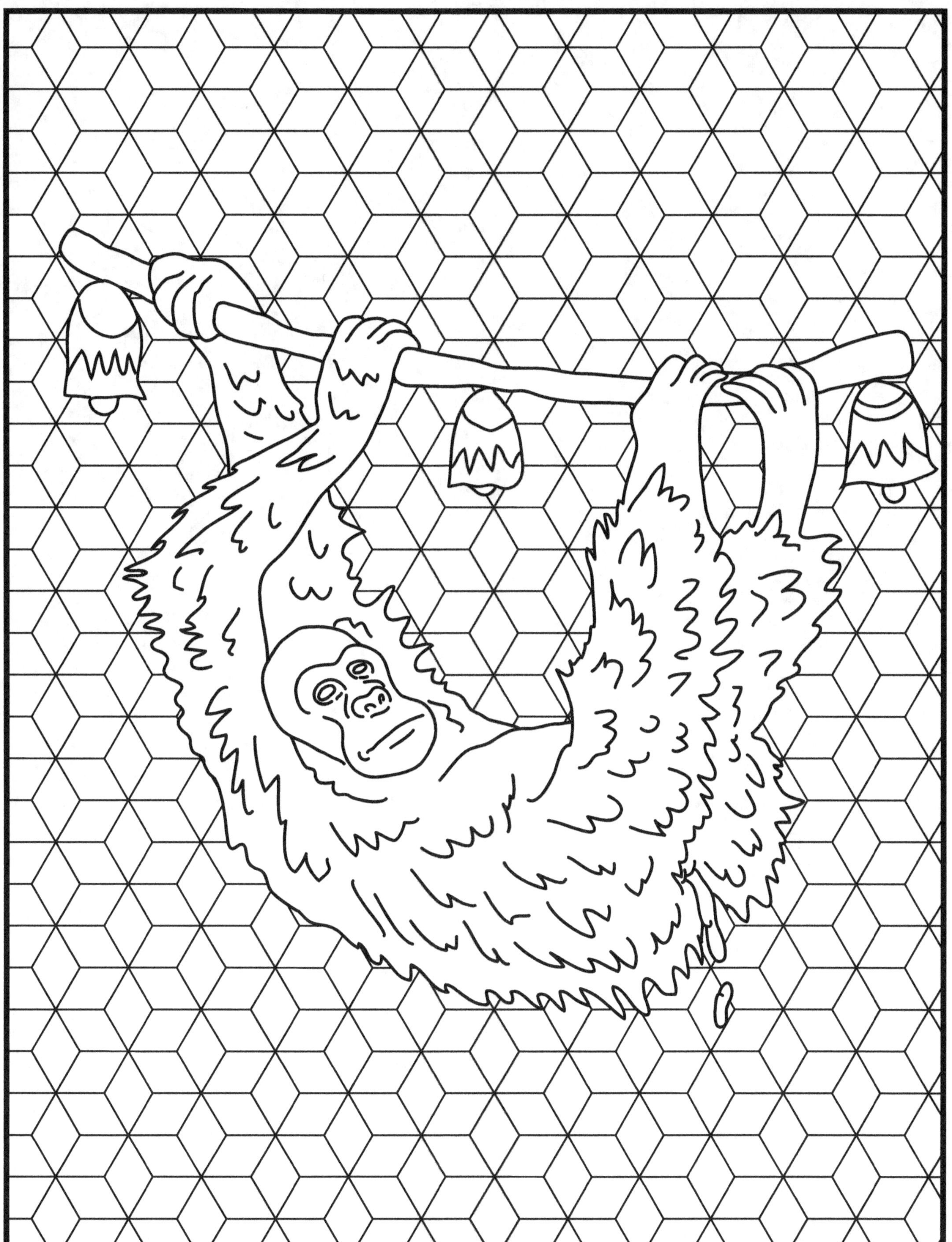

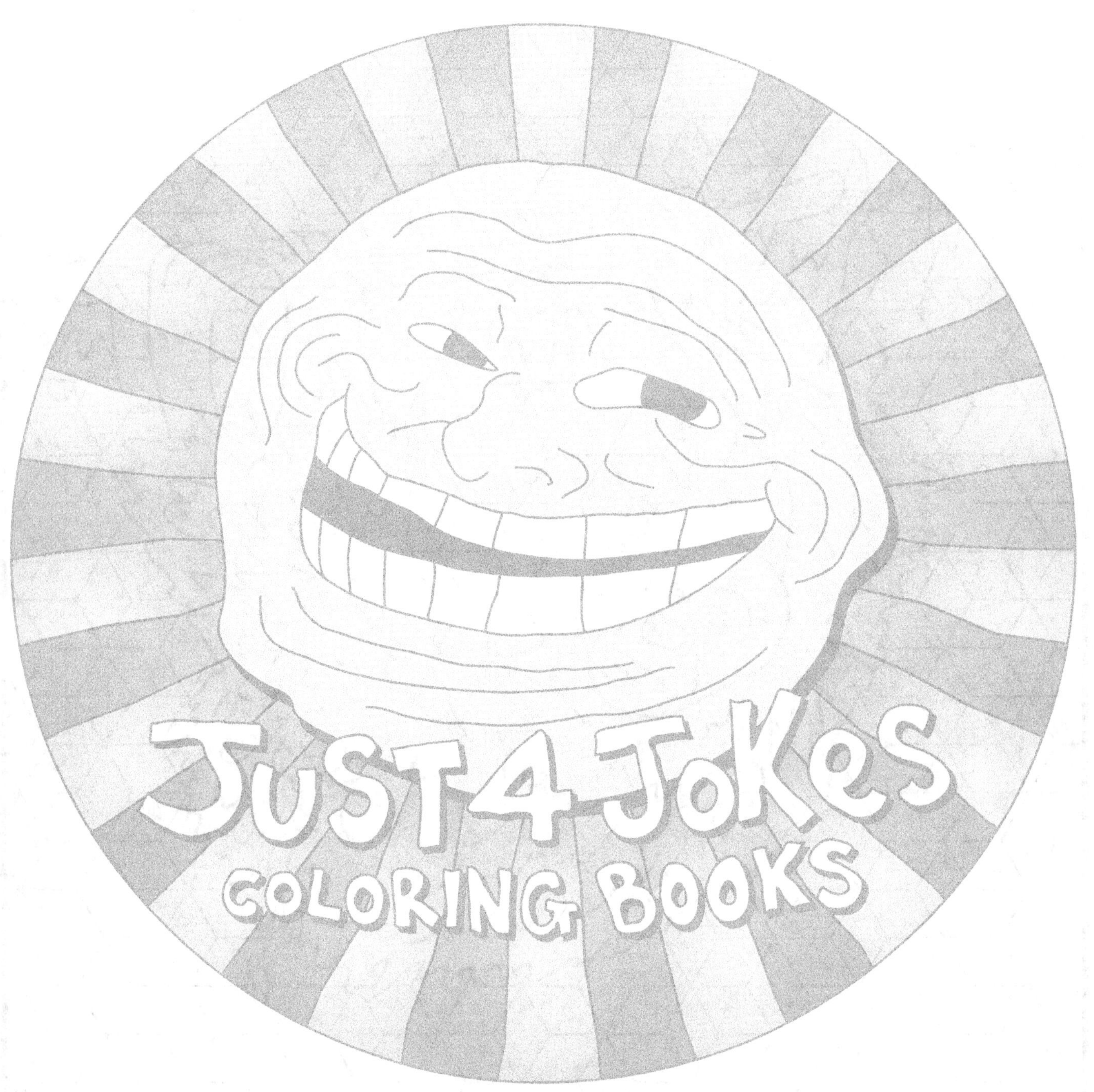

JUST 4 JOKES
COLORING BOOKS

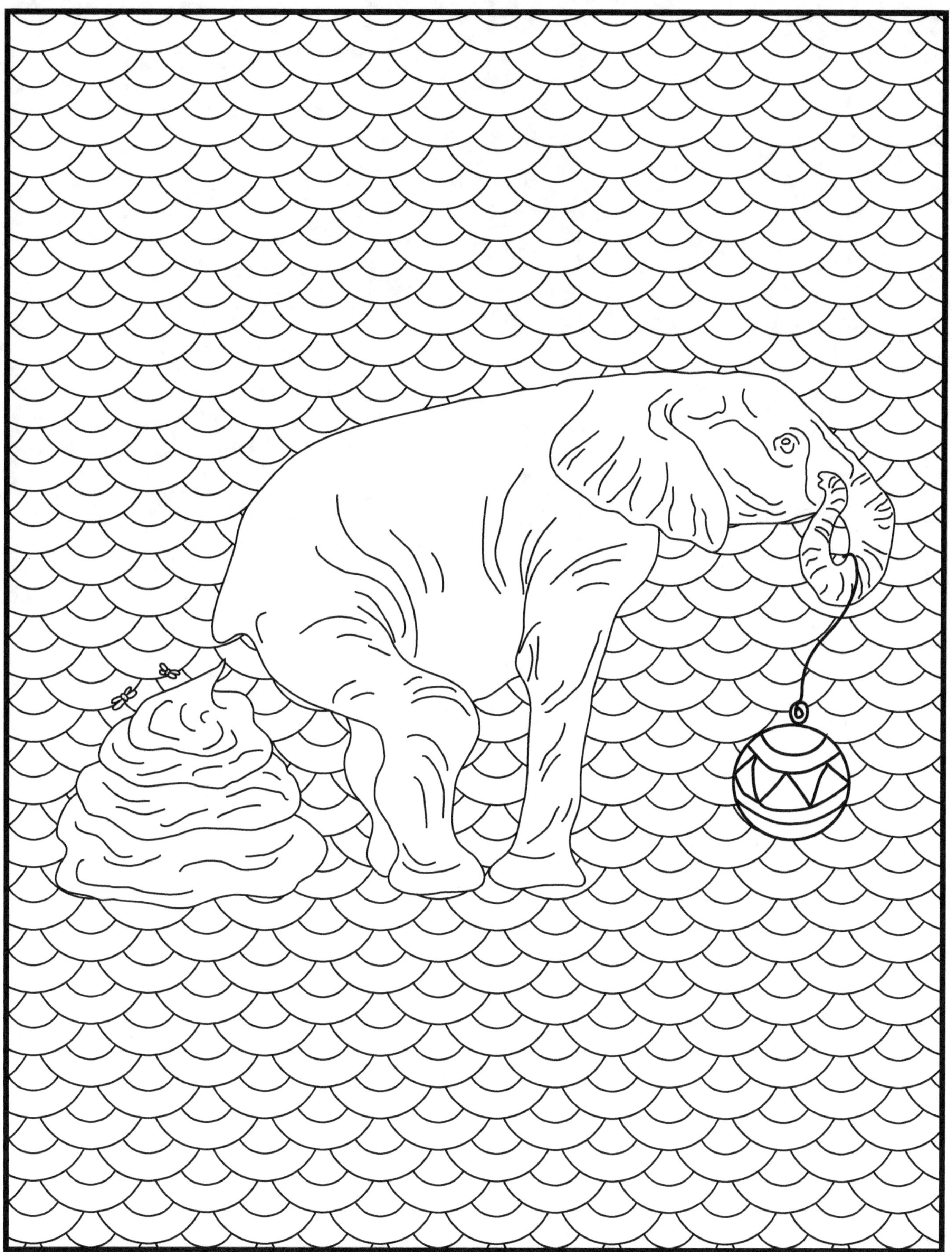

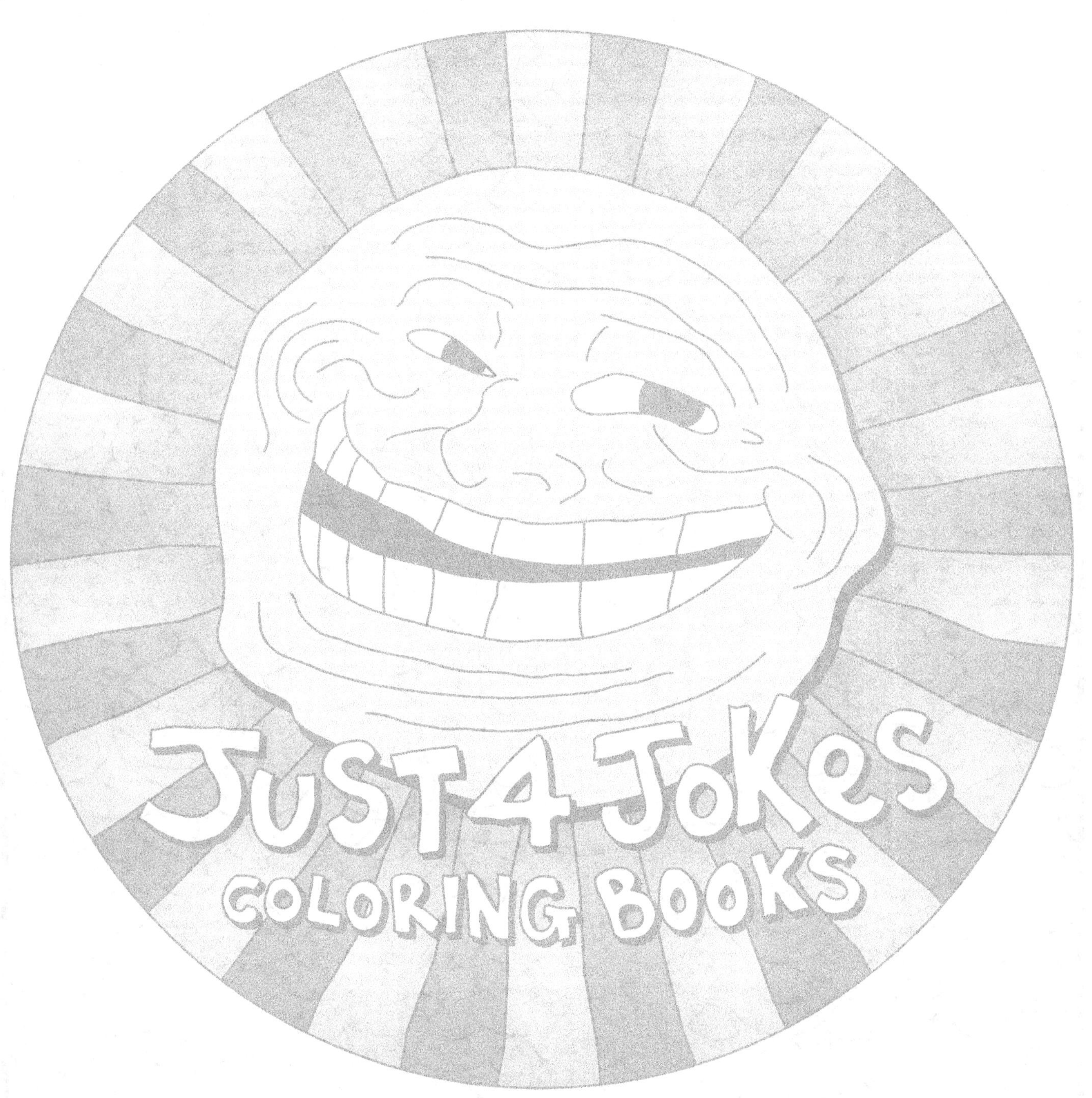

JUST 4 JOKES
COLORING BOOKS

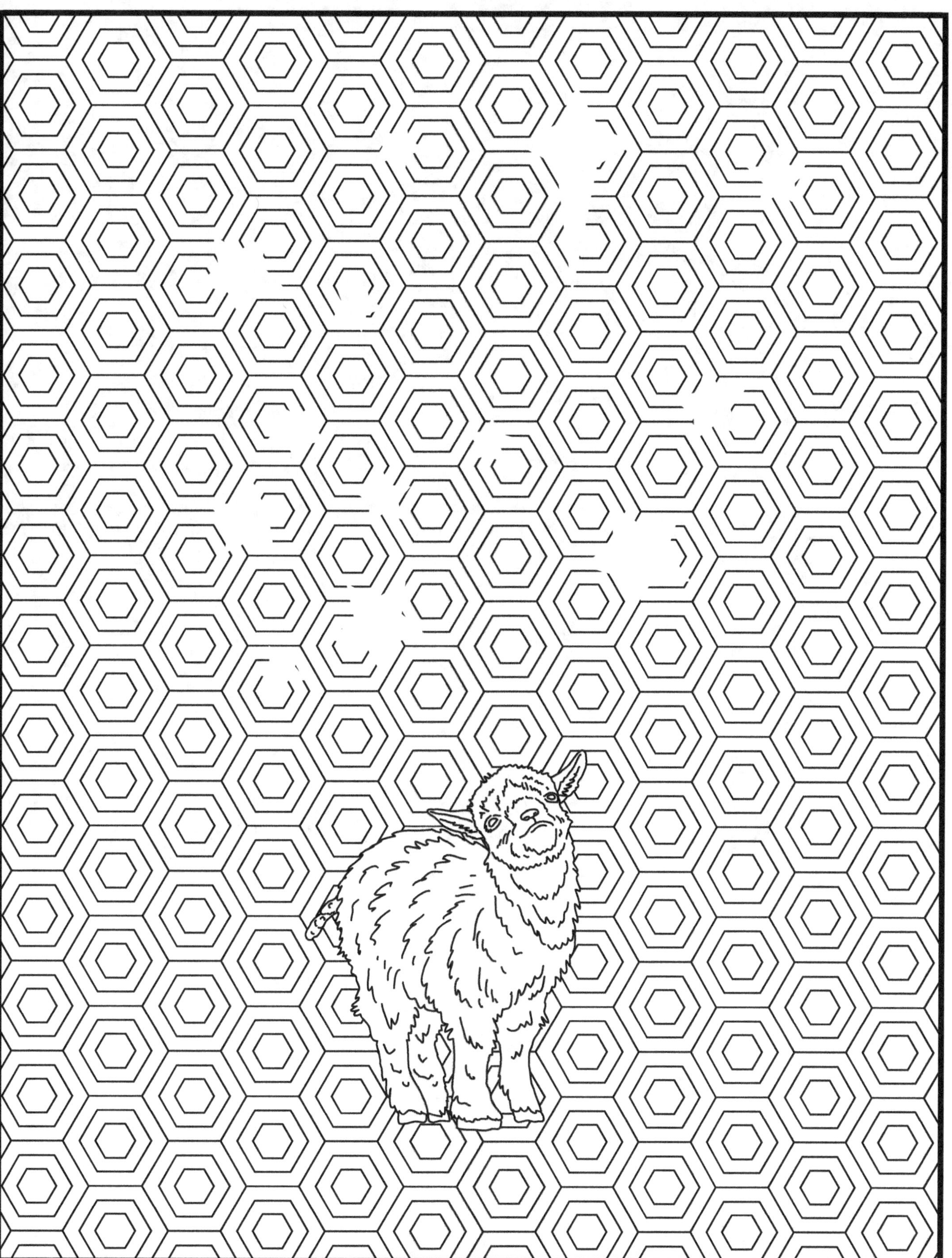

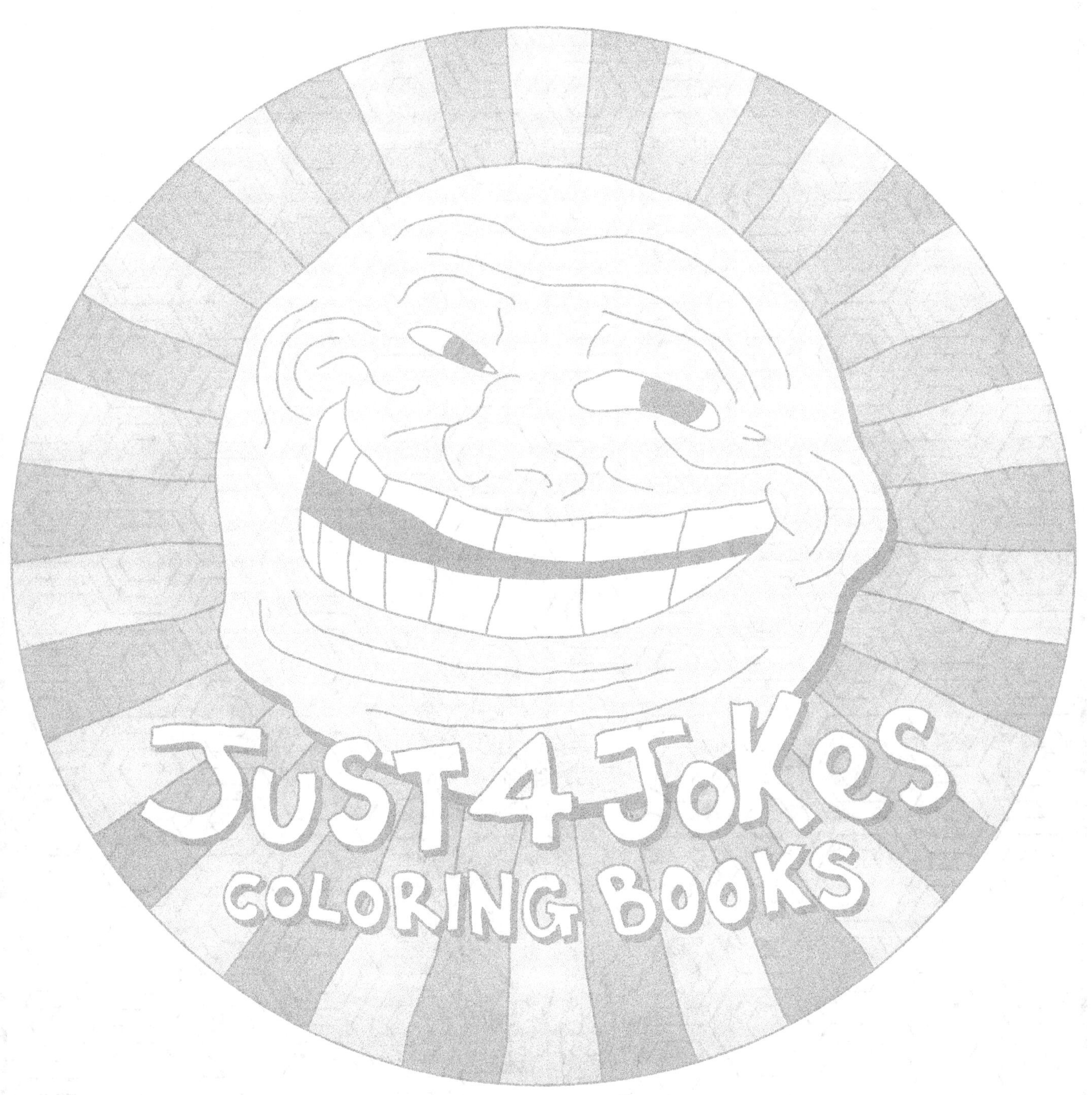

JUST4JOKES
COLORING BOOKS

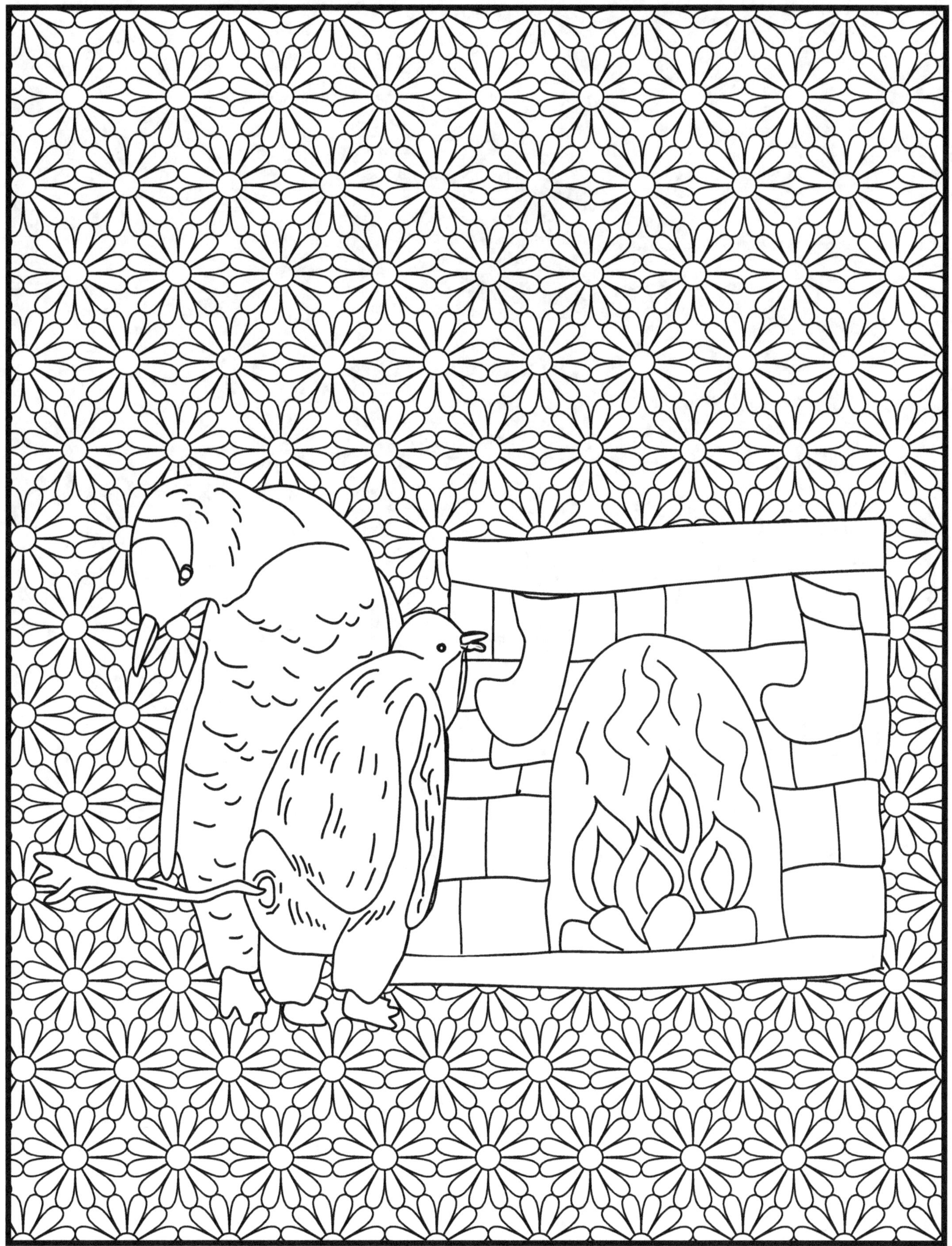

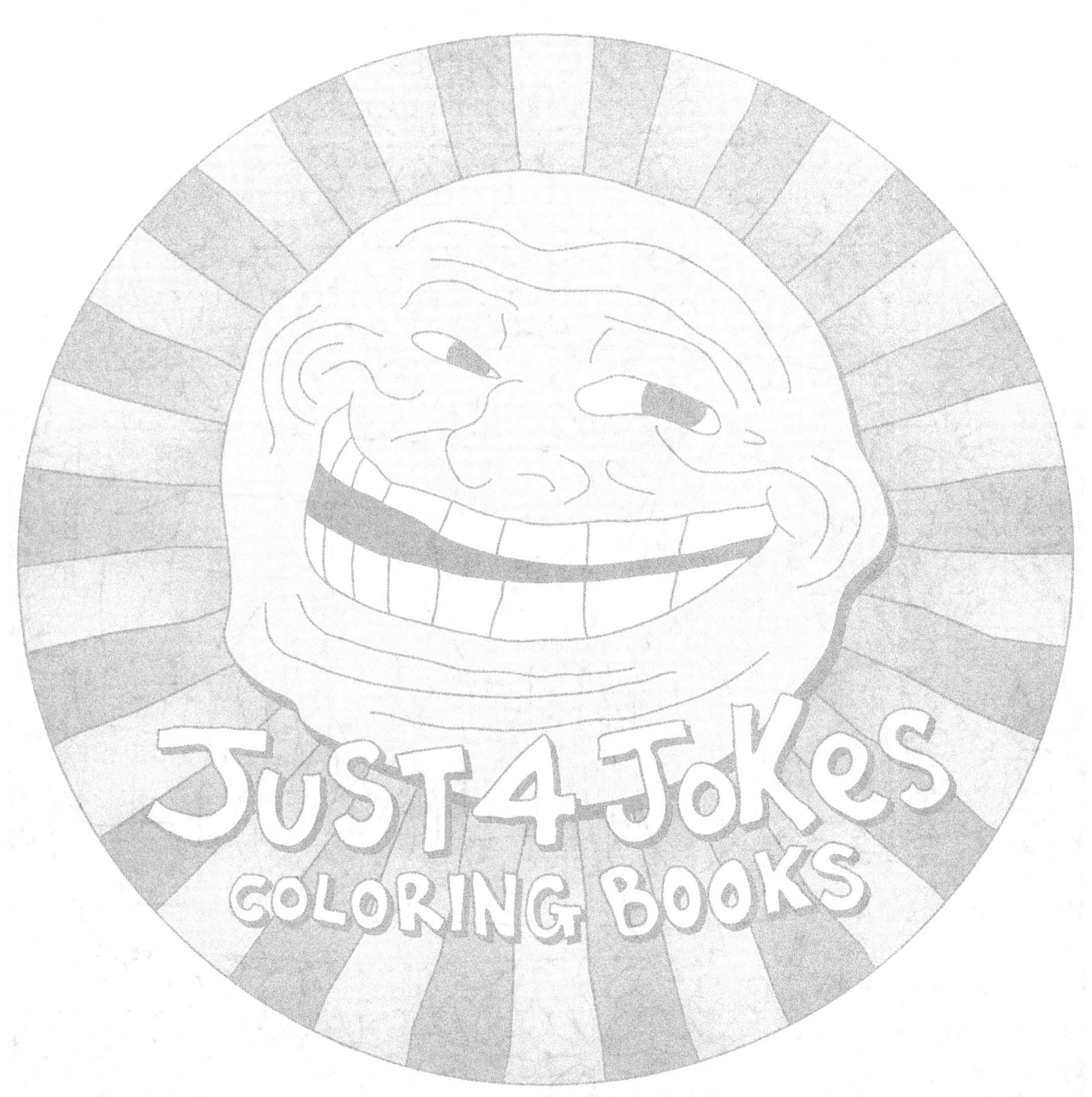
JUST 4 JOKES
COLORING BOOKS

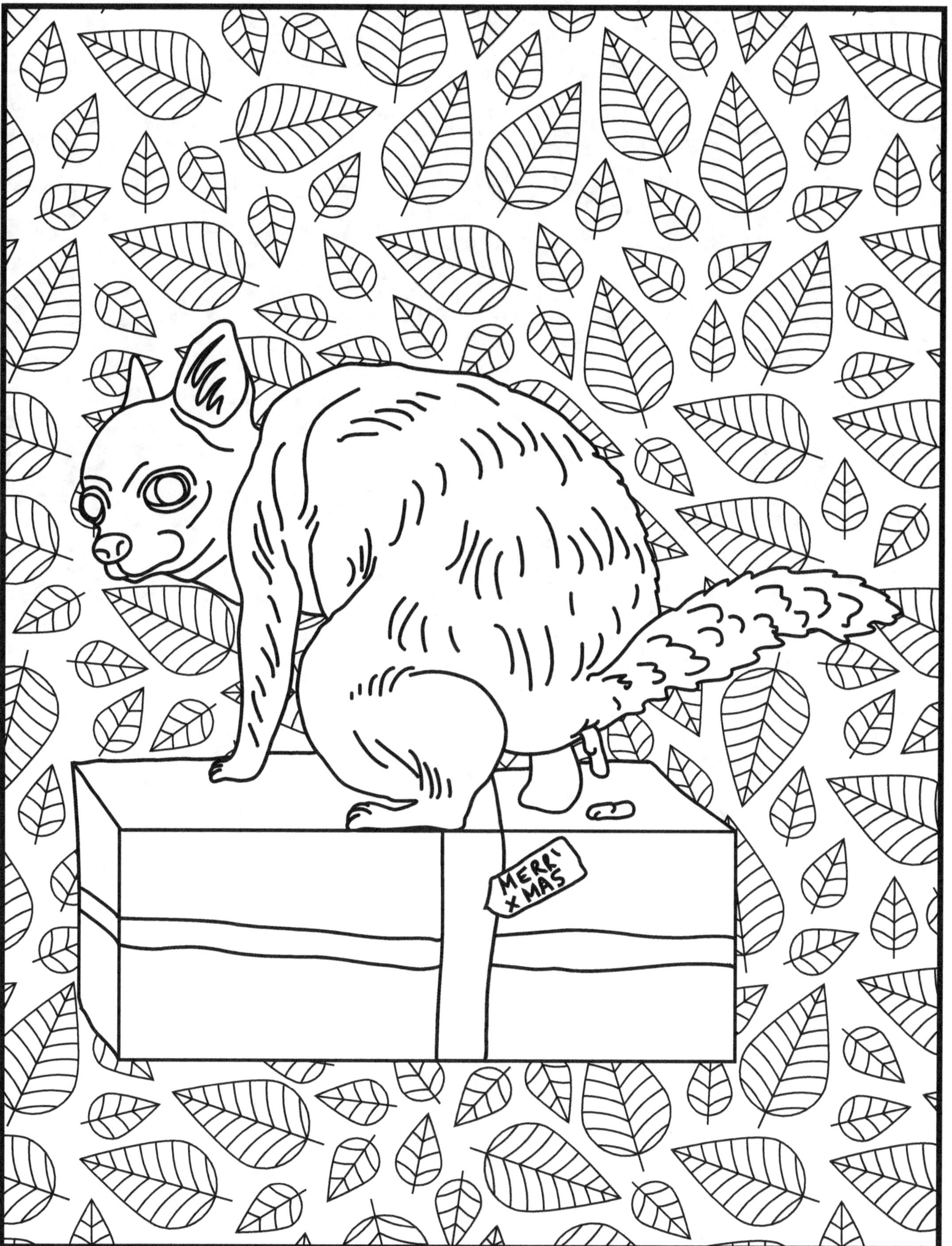
MERR'
X MAS

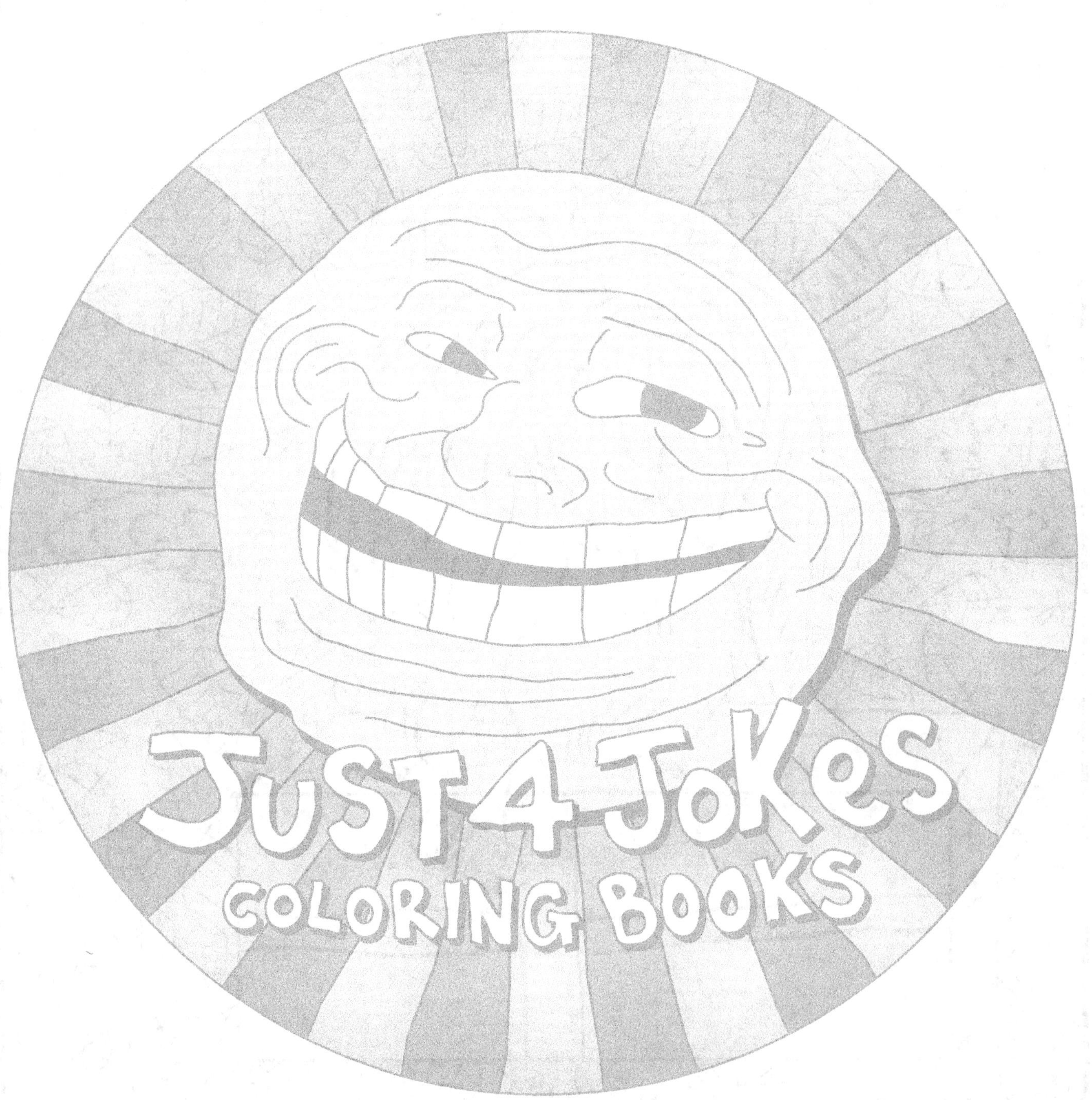

Just4Jokes
COLORING BOOKS

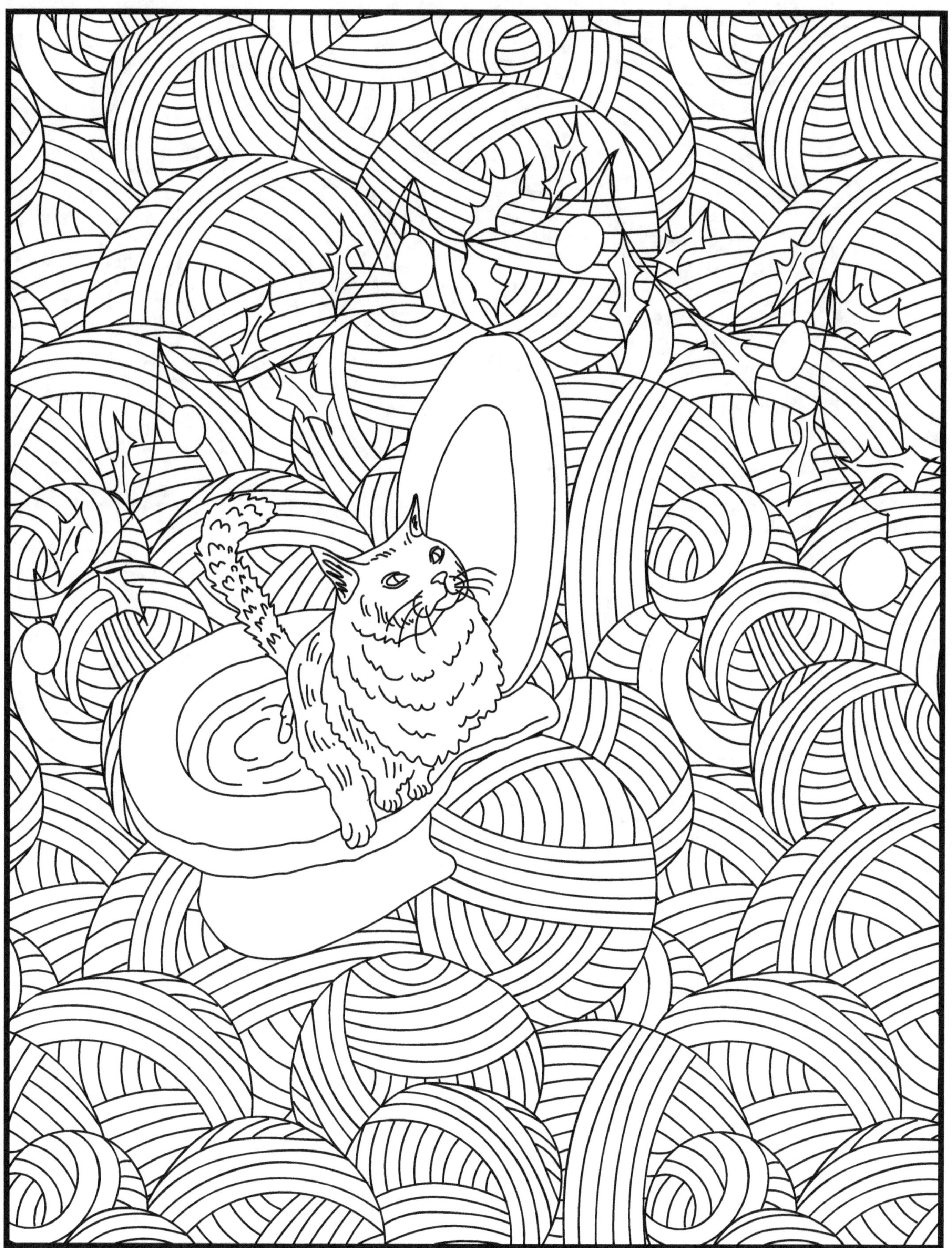

JUST 4 JOKES
COLORING BOOKS

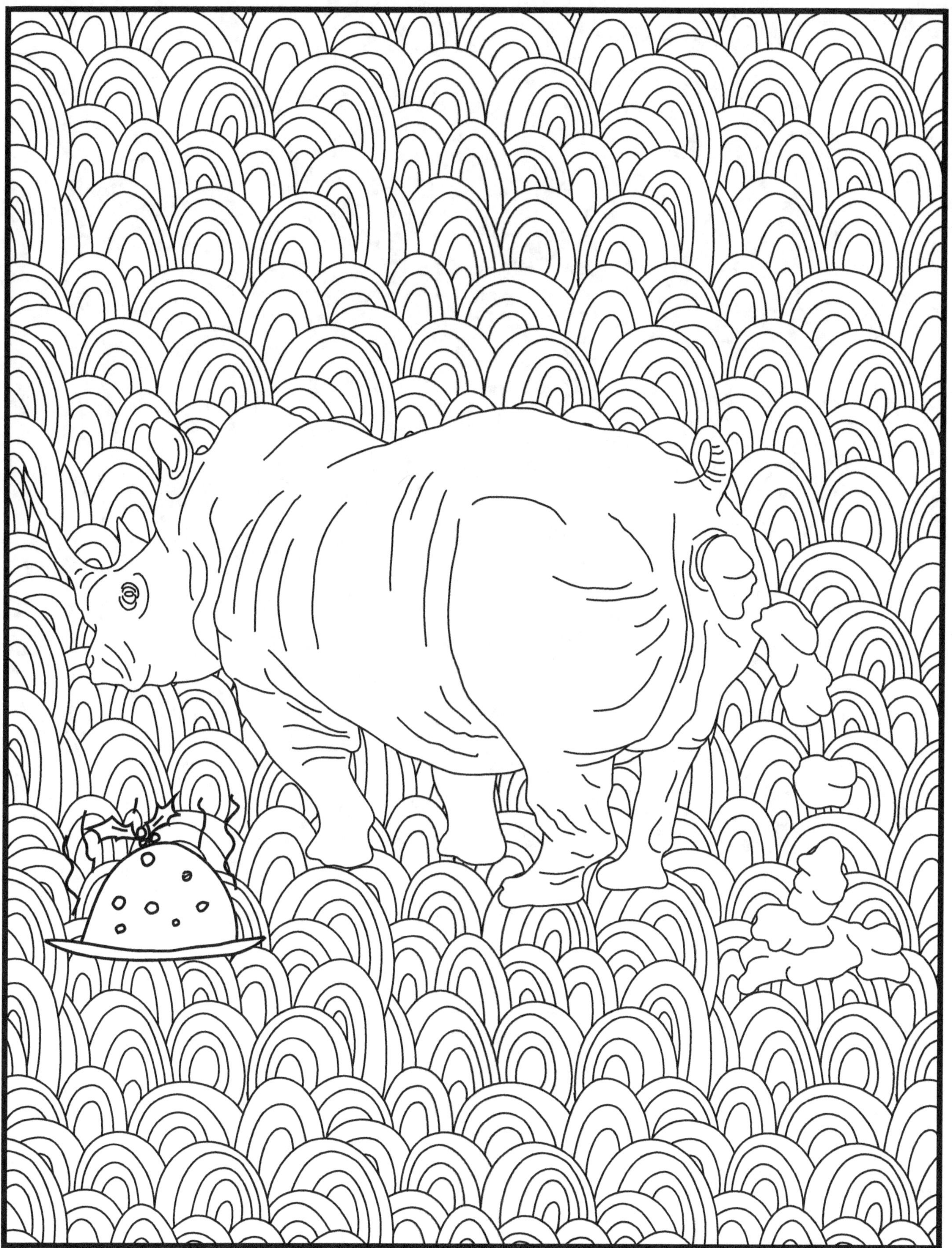

JUST 4 JOKES
COLORING BOOKS

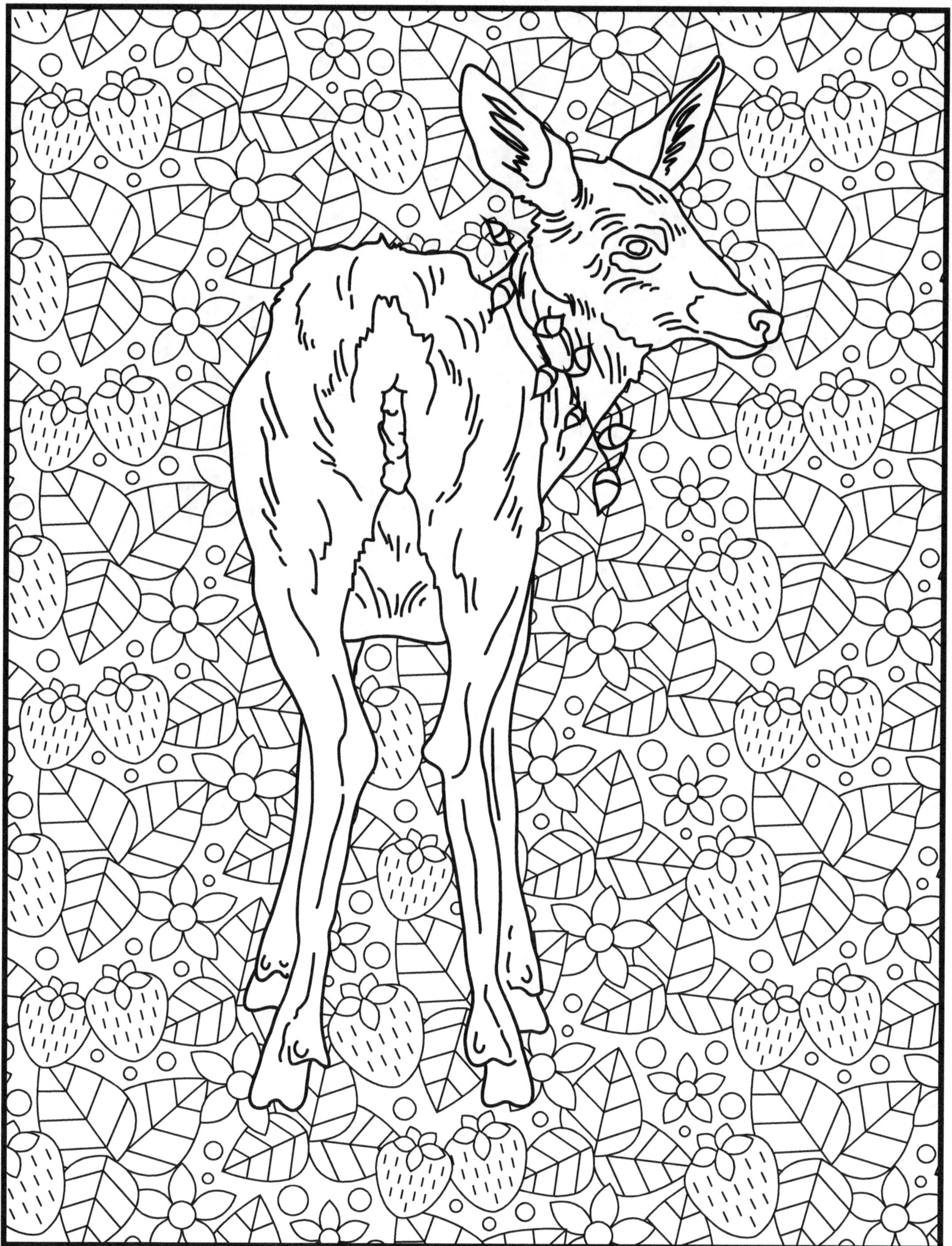

Just 4 Jokes
Coloring Books

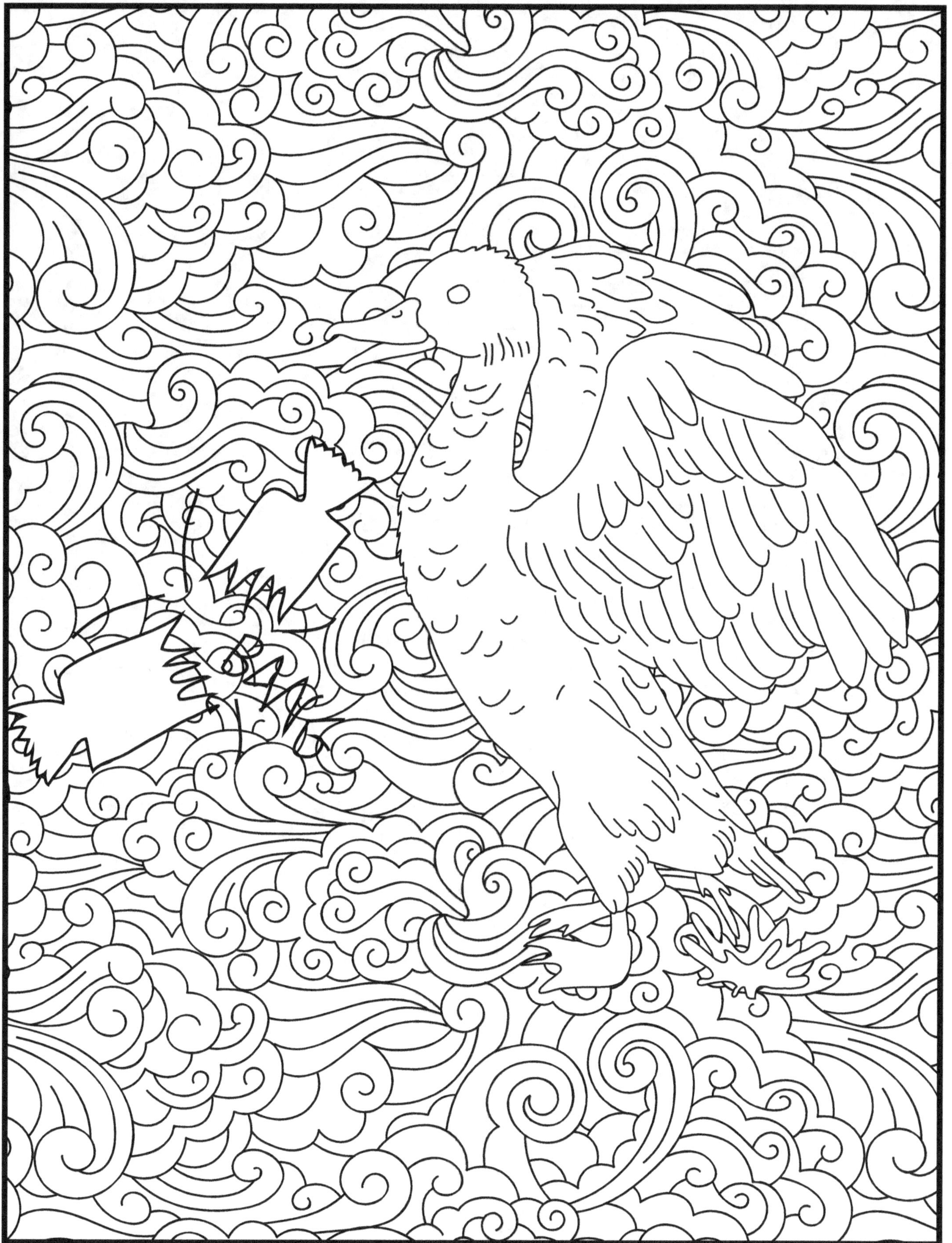

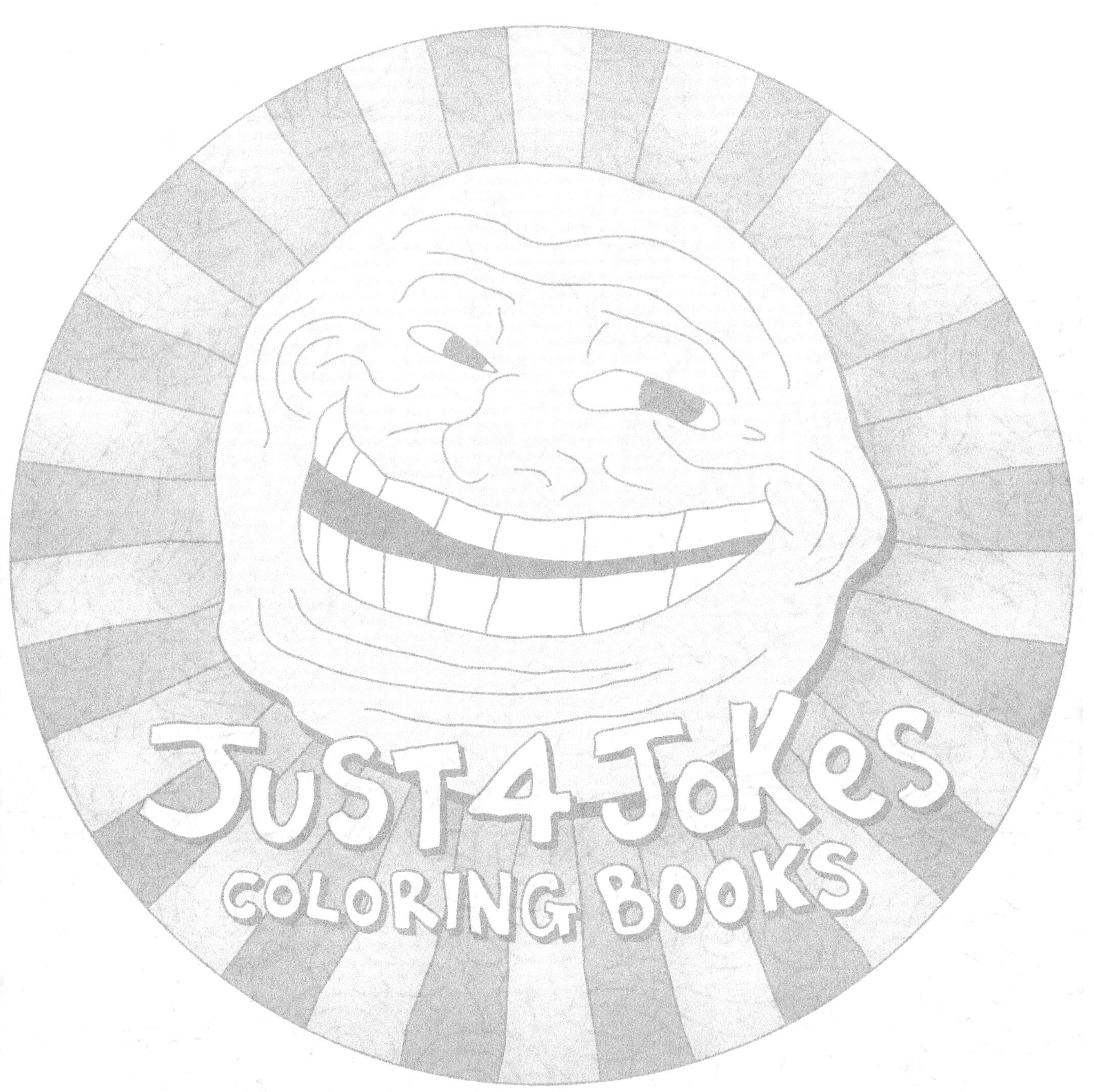
JUST 4 JOKES
COLORING BOOKS

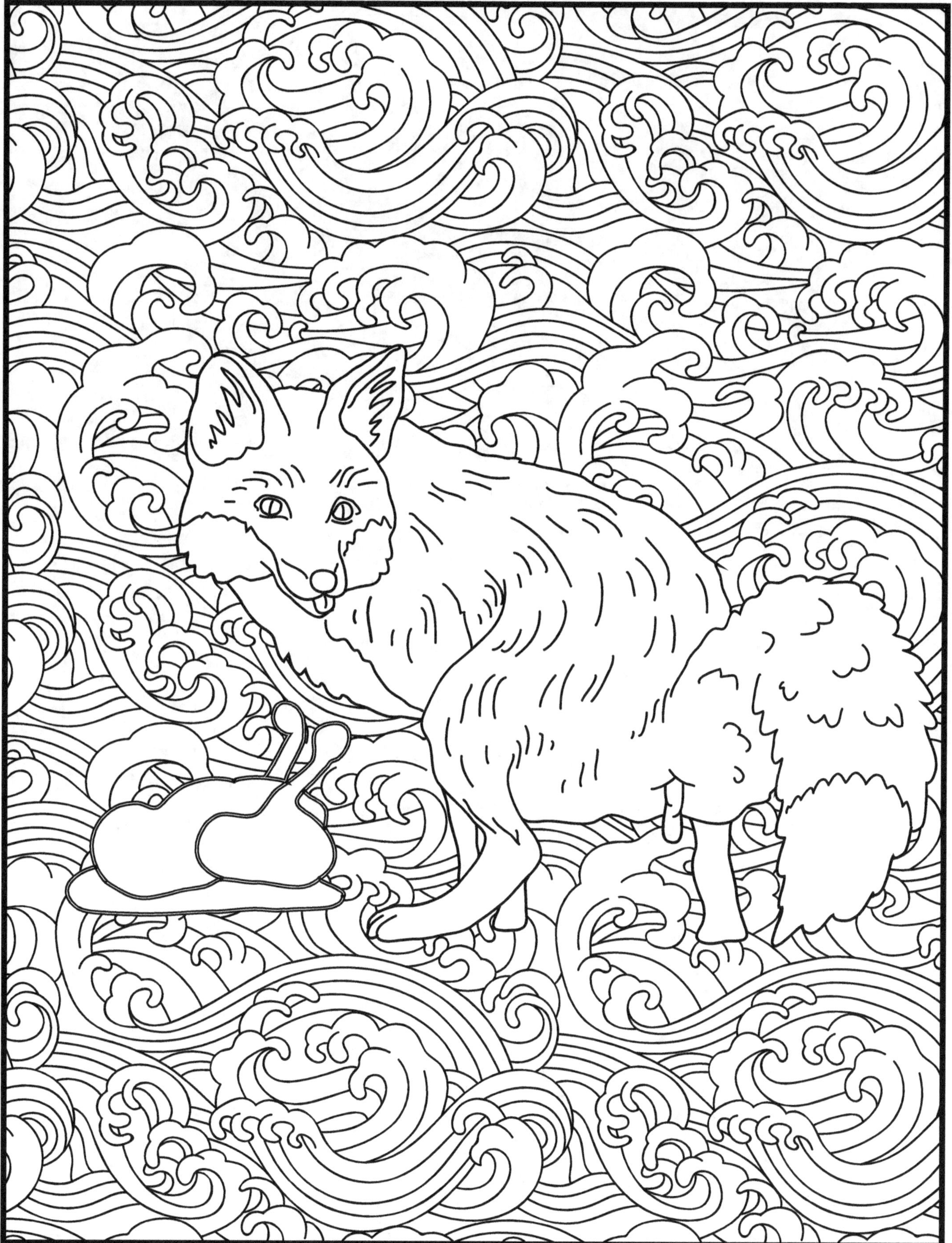

JUST 4 JOKES
COLORING BOOKS

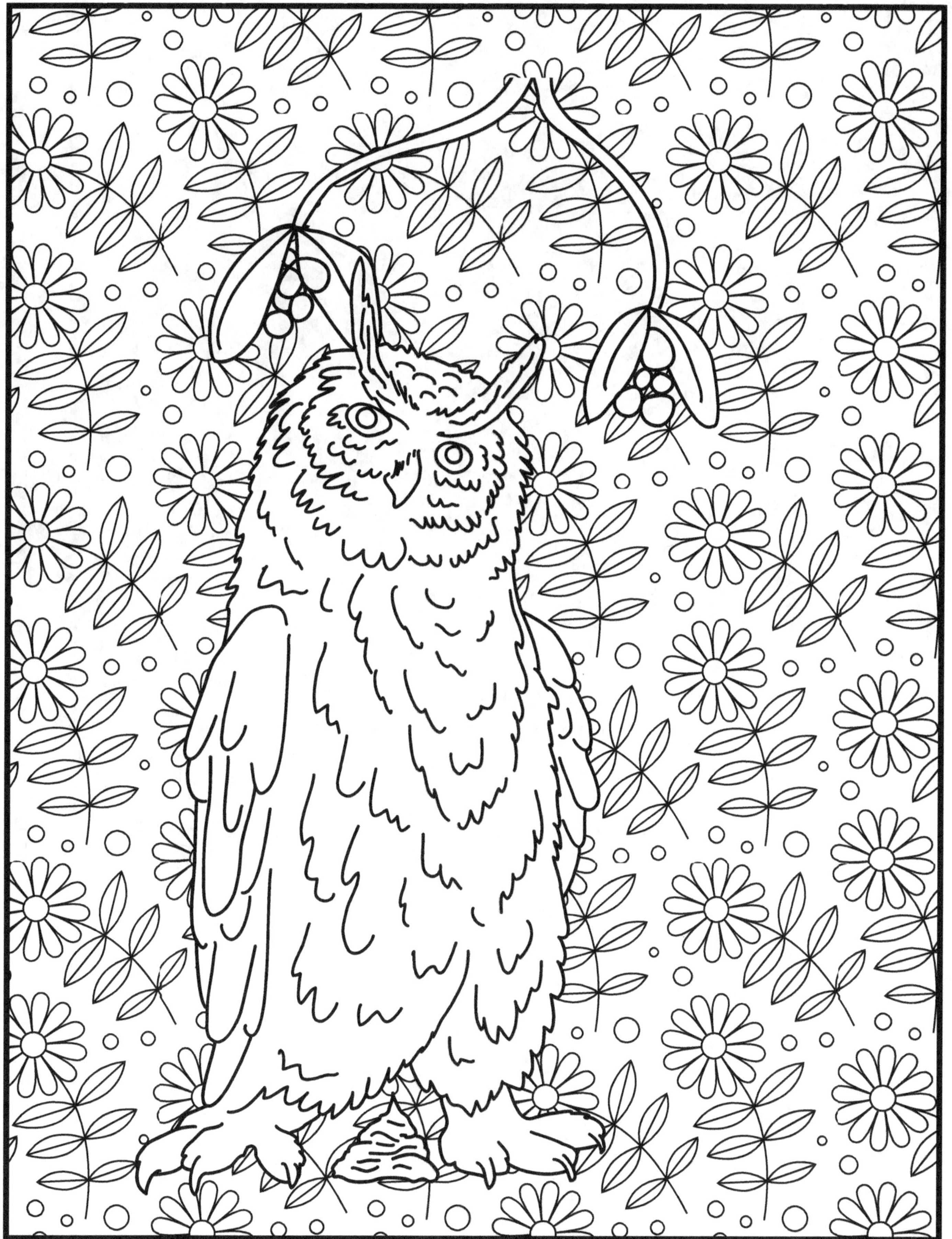

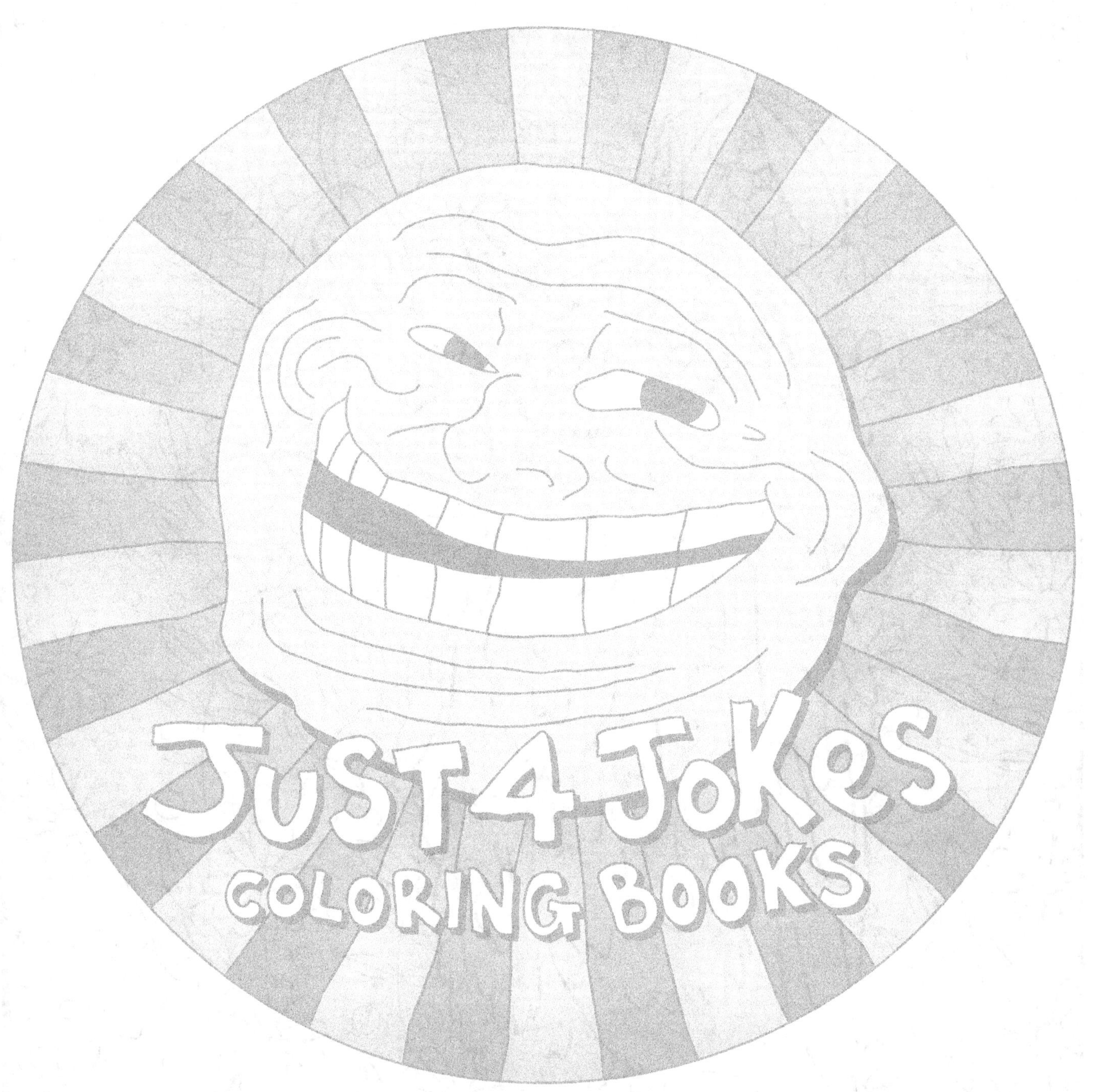

Just 4 Jokes
Coloring Books

Color Test Page

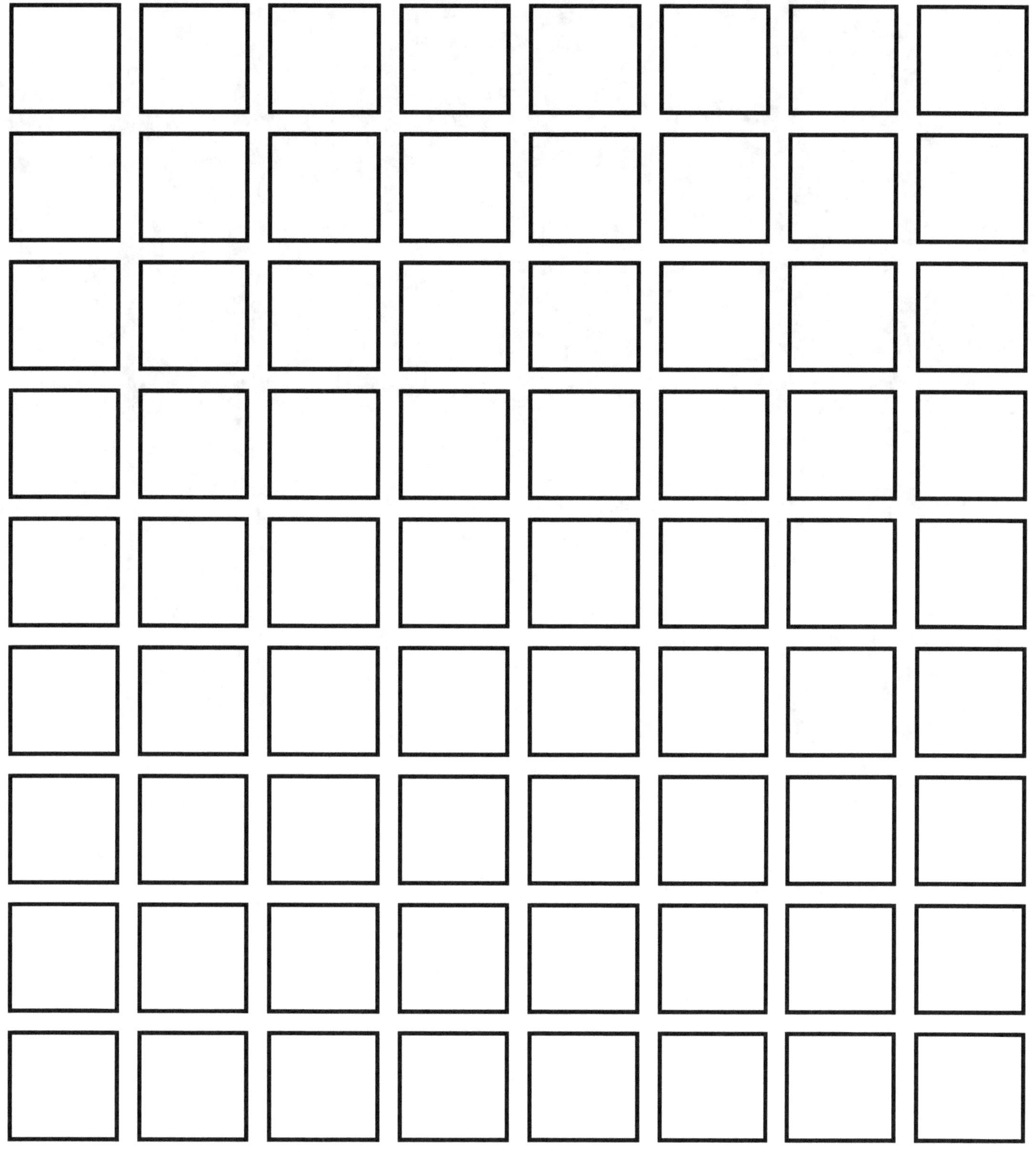

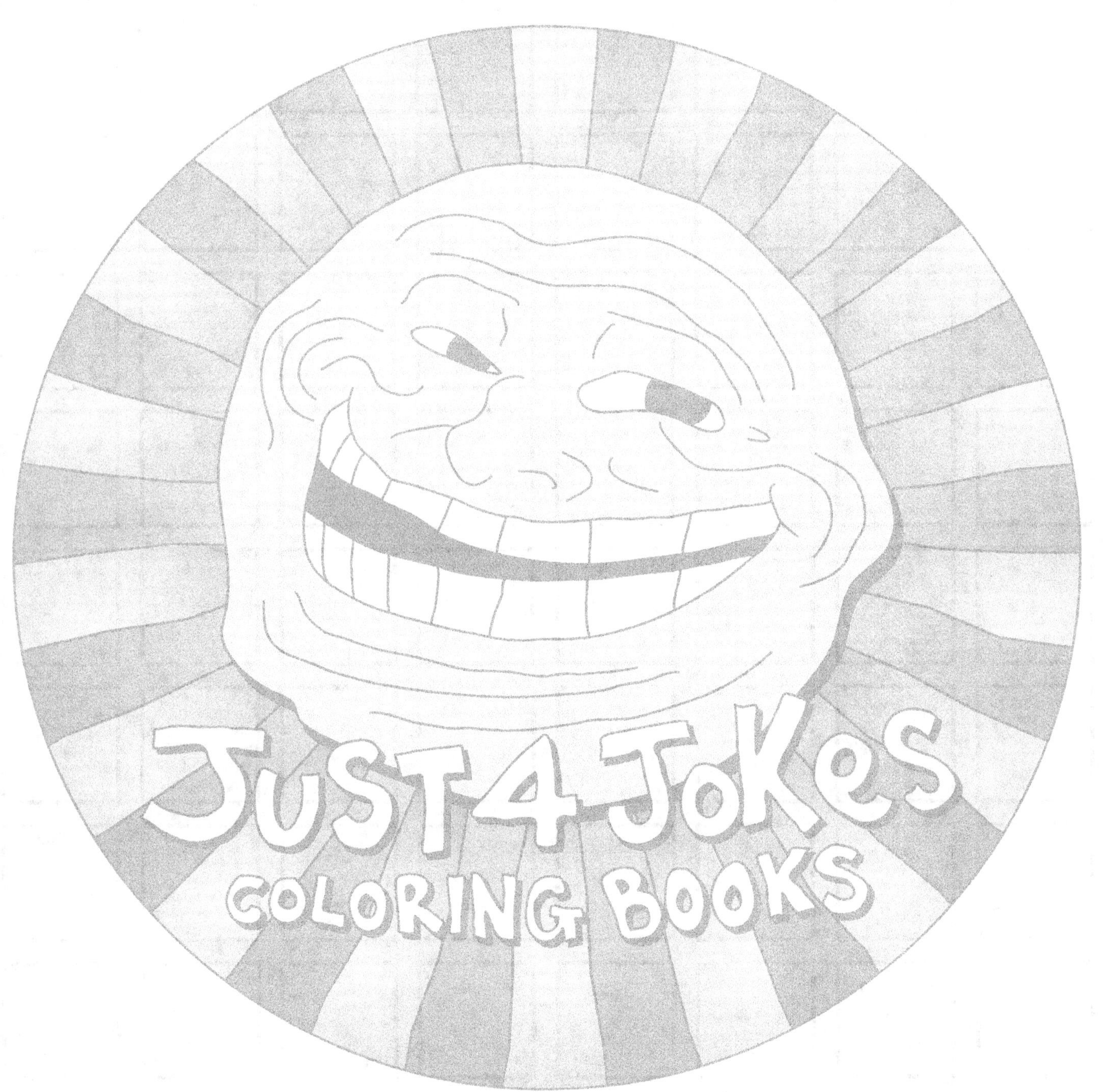

JUST4JOKES
COLORING BOOKS

Color Test Page

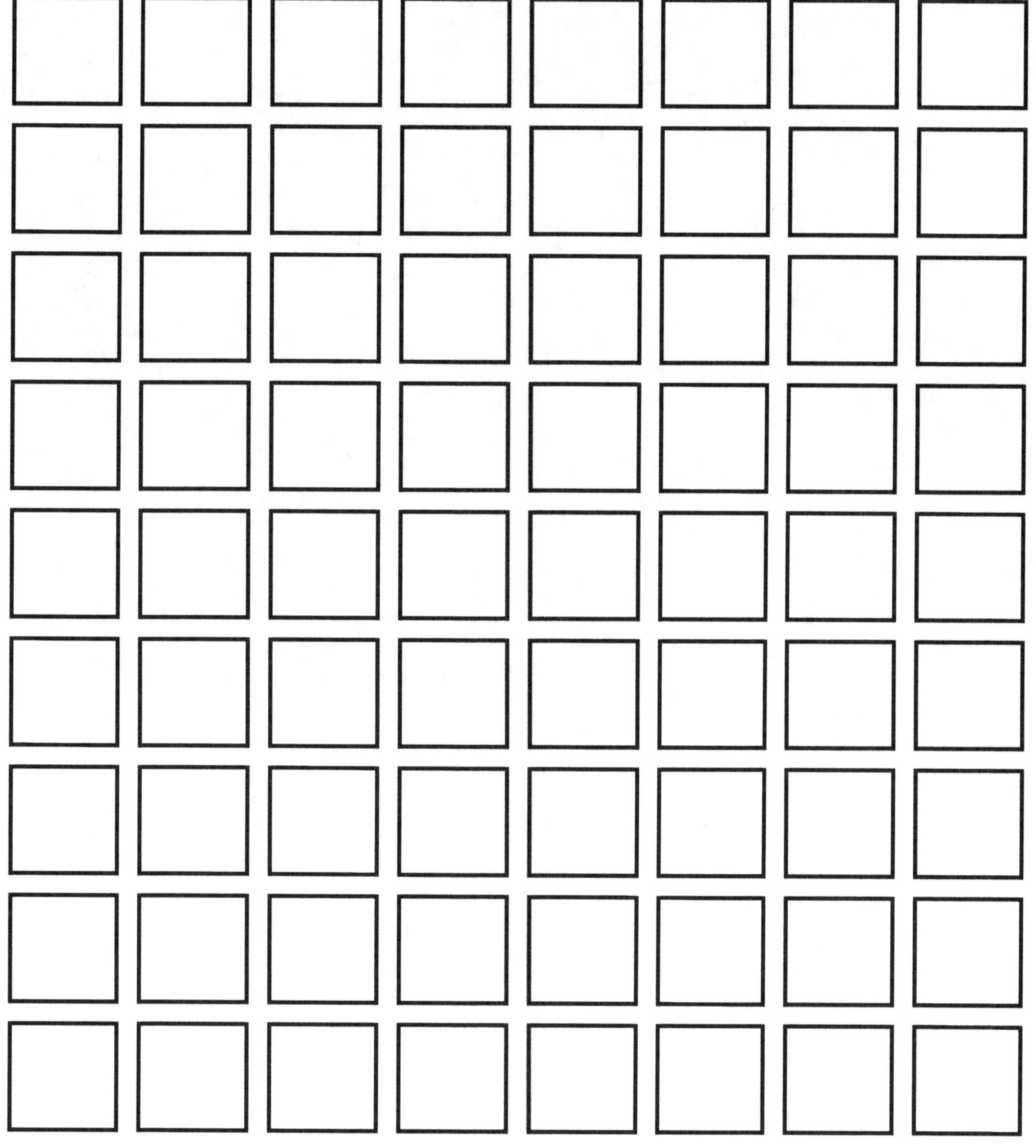

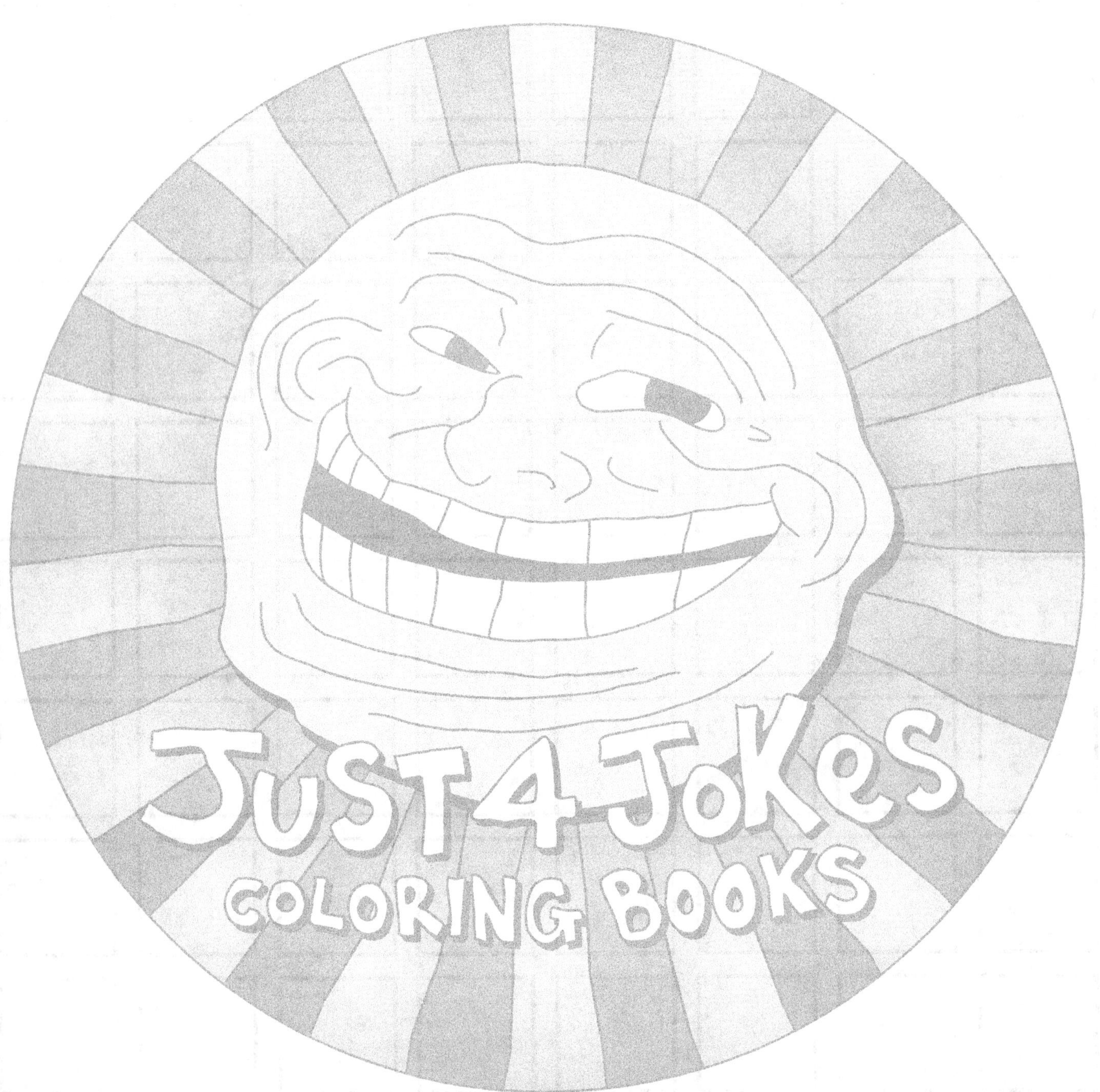

JusT 4 JoKes
COLORING BOOKS